TRAVELS WITH MY MOTHER

TRAVELS WITH MY MOTHER

PETER CALDER

TANDEM PRESS

First published in New Zealand in 2003 by
TANDEM PRESS
PO Box 34 272
Birkenhead, Auckland
New Zealand
www.tandempress.co.nz

Reprinted 2003, 2004 (twice)

National Library of New Zealand Cataloguing-in-Publication Data

Calder, Peter, 1952-
Travels with my mother / Peter Calder.
ISBN 1-877298-09-3
Calder, Peter, 1952—Childhood and youth. 2. Calder, Peter, 1952—Travel—England. 3. Mothers and sons. 4. New Zealand—Social life and customs. I. Title.
305.823092—dc 21

Cover and text design by Jacinda Torrance / Verso
Production by Cara Torrance / Pen to Paper
Printed in New Zealand by Publishing Press Ltd

For Mum, of course.

INTRODUCTION

We all want to know where we came from. The problem is that we assume it's a place, when it's something much more complicated than that.

Last year I took my 82-year-old mother to England. We went, like the pussy cat, 'up to London to visit the Queen'. But it was a longer journey, too, along the streets her maternal forebears travelled as they left Penzance in Cornwall to take ship for New Zealand.

The visit to one's roots is a New Zealand rite of passage, something young New Zealanders doing their OE might fit in on a wet weekend between working in London and backpacking around Europe. The OE of my youth ground to a halt somewhere in the Andes and turned into an extended tour of duty in Latin America. I never made London until the 1990s.

This was an altogether different journey. One who has always enjoyed travelling alone, I found myself travelling for, as well as with, someone else. I was babysitter and tour guide, driver and luggage carrier. I was adult; she was child.

But it was not all hard work. It was my journey, too, a trip as much internal as external. In visiting the Englishman I might have been, I learnt more about the New Zealander I became.

In accomplishing this objective, I was enthusiastically and generously supported by the Auckland office of the British Tourist Authority. Maggie Hunt and Paul Petersen warmed instantly to the idea of helping and made it their mission to ensure that the client they knew as 'Mumsy' had the trip of a lifetime. Their extraordinary professionalism and good humour during the trying process of planning the trip – not once but twice – lightened my load immeasurably. The support of Air New Zealand who provided me with a round-trip ticket is also gratefully acknowledged.

Bob Ross and Helen Benton of Tandem Press were enormously encouraging when an author who had never written anything longer than 5000 words was daunted by the scale of the task in front of him. Their constant sense of what the book was was no small help during the periods when I lost sight of it.

But this is, first and foremost, the record of my mother's achievement. She was a gutsy and plucky travelling companion who endured without complaint the pain of pounding the pavements or keeping up to the demands of an itinerary. It was fun to see the world through her eyes. And, even when moved to scrawl 'This is rubbish!' in the margins of the manuscript, she never lost sight of the fact that this wasn't necessarily what happened; it was just what I wrote.

To be an Englishman is to belong to the most exclusive club there is.
– Ogden Nash

There is a new religion – the type that sees colonials beetling through ancestral relics and documentation. The impulse to know who our great grandparents were is a profound impulse, an instinctive tendency towards ancestor worship – a natural religion, almost genetic. We reinvigorate our imagination by finding our ghosts, even if they were a crazy pack of bastards.
– Thomas Keneally

HOME THOUGHTS FROM ABROAD

I always fancied myself as a crazy bastard. I wanted to strike fear into the hearts of men by my excess of spirit. I would drink in small bars – no, shebeens, or bistrots rather – or in corner cafés where dark wood tables and tiled walls reeked of a hundred thousand wild nights before me, danced away by men with unpronounceable names and forebears who were hunters or winemakers or woodsmen.

I would drink rustic reds or beer in ceramic steins or drain shot glasses of clear firewater served by sullen waiters in black with shin-length white aprons. I would pour out – or be poured out – well after midnight into a moonlit market square.

In this city I would be a poet, composing impenetrable but plainly subversive verse, which was published on coarse-woven hand-made paper in thin volumes whose page-edges were torn raggedly with a letter-knife and which no one ever bought or understood. I would appear, scowling, at the same – no, a different – café for a late, haggard breakfast of croissants and bowls of sweet, milky coffee.

I would smoke, heavily, cigarettes of cheap dark tobacco, which I would fish from a crushed pack. No matter how ill-advised my habits, I would be indestructible.

I would have a passionate relationship with the postmistress, a raven-haired young widow with whom, it would be rumoured, I was carrying on even before her husband had died.

Instead, I am walking along Boundary Road in Hamilton past the marshalling yards of the showgrounds and the hydatids dosing strip. My belly is full of Kornies and banana and creamy Waikato milk. I am wearing a dark Sunday suit, a hand-me-down two sizes too large. It is summer, the end of the 1950s, and I swelter in the ringingly bright sunlight and dawdle.

Beyond the yard, across the dry-mud races pocked with hoof marks and rutted with the tyres of horse floats, where the cracked concrete heaves and swells around the fence posts in the heat, the Huntly brick of St Aidan's basks, blond and banal.

There is no wildness here. Neat, orderly Hamilton is a place where predictability is both an asset and an aspiration. This second wave of settlers at mid-century are turning what has always been a depot town for the surrounding dairy country into a little slice of England.

Here in the belly of Tainui, the newcomers plant hedgerows and prune roses and leave enough room on the quarter-acre for a cricket pitch. And on Sundays, even as the island's centre winces in the heat of mid-summer, they roast a piece of the fat of this land.

That midday meal is now the business of the three dark-suited boys who are walking home ahead of parents delayed by a vestry meeting.

We're not often together like this, the three of us. My two brothers are usually away at boarding school in Auckland, where they are learning to be little Englishmen abroad and to answer to names that distinguish them as Calders Major and Minor. Resplendent in heavy red cassocks and Persil-white surplices, they sing in a choir conceived to replicate perfectly the one at another, more legendary King's College.

They are mostly about big boys' business, all hairy legs and hard swot and sweaty sports and no dawdling. To amble home like this is my speciality, and I glow with the pride of ownership of this expedition while taking care to keep the fact well hidden from the others.

Our mission – to 'check the roast' – really is an awesome responsibility. The kitchen, after all, is Mum's domain and only in extraordinary circumstances is anyone else entitled to do anything there. 'Checking the roast', like cooking it, was always Mum's job. The Vanguard would barely have come to a halt; its motor would still be clicking cool in the garage as she bustled in, pulling off her gloves and hurrying to the oven where the joint had been quietly baking since we left.

This was before they had invented barbecues or alfresco dining. Those were heathen (read Catholic) practices. We rehearsed the domestic habits of our forebears, Celtic folk –

Scottish highlanders, Yorkshire mothers and Cornish carpenters – with pale skin not made for this harsh sun.

This was food fit for a banquet in a land where the snow piled around the door and the wild wind worried at the chimney pot above the cooking fire. But we carved the fat (and the lean) of the land from a sticky charred bone each Sunday for lunch even when the heat haze rose like a hallucination from the paddocks behind the house.

It was in the hallway, outside a room of Wellington's James Cook hotel, that the idea was born. I looked out over the tops of office blocks on Lambton Quay, as a southerly kicked up whitecaps on the inner harbour, and wondered.

In the anonymous surroundings of the room, we had been filling toothbrush tumblers and minibar beer glasses with wine poured from bottles still in their paper bags, and drinking a toast to my Uncle Geoff, whose shrunken body we had just farewelled at Old St Paul's in Thorndon.

As wakes go, it was a small and sober affair; but it was full of good humour as we reminisced about the last months of a life ended by Alzheimer's disease. My 80-year-old mother, the deceased's only sibling, was scrambling to keep up, wiping a tear from her eye and wistfully recalling things that had never happened in order to join in the fun. For all of us it was a process of trying to tame the memories that spread like a stain over the last few years.

We had watched a meticulously organised mind slowly sinking into the blackness of senility. But now that he was gone, we could afford to laugh at the fretful forgetfulness, the eccentric habits that took over as dementia began fraying the neat edges of his accountant's mind.

The *New Zealand Herald*, for which I had written for almost 20 years, had been a part of Geoff's morning for something like sixty. Towards the end, I recalled, he had defied the disorder, reading the paper with a dogged resolve to defy the encroaching darkness. With a pen in hand, he would strike out each paragraph with an oblique stroke as it passed before his glazing eyes.

He would, of course, instantly forget what he had just read. Like sun-struck mist on a lake, the awareness of it would vanish so fast it had no time to attain the status of memory. But his ingestion of the morning paper was a civic duty and he continued to read it even when he had no real idea of what it all meant.

Geoff had always venerated the newspaper, regarding it as something close to holy writ. As he saw it, my position as one of the paper's staff writers entitled me to consideration for a Nobel Prize. He would occasionally send letters to the editor singing my praises, and these would be forwarded to me in the house mail with 'A relative, I presume' scrawled at the bottom in the editor's snide red pen.

Yet in his last years, as we took afternoon tea in the kiosk at Cornwall Park, he struggled to remember where he had met me before.

Immaculately turned out in tweed jacket and tie, even on warm summer afternoons, he would scan the plates on the table, trying to work out where to lay the butter knife in his hand. 'Who are you again?' he would ask, laying it carefully in the sugar bowl. And then, when I told him: 'Of course you are. And what do you do?'

The last time I saw him, I took him for a cup of tea in the lounge of the rest home where he had spent his last, grey widower years, while upstairs his son and daughter, my cousins, sorted through his few possessions. He was being taken to Wellington to another rest home, within easier visiting distance of children and grandchildren. He sat opposite me, thin and sallow, his liver-spotted hands fretting at the brim of his plaid hat. Our conversation was a looping, circular thing that might have been written by Beckett or Ionesco.

'I'm sorry, Peter,' he would say with a worried frown, 'but I can't make head or tail of this.'

'You're going to Wellington, Geoff,' I'd tell him.

His eyes bulged, comically wide with wonder.

'To Wellington!' he'd explode, before sinking into a ruminative silence for a few moments. Then: 'Where did you say I was going?'

'To Wellington, Geoff.'

'When?'

'Today. At 12 o'clock.'

'Today?' The tone was one of horror. 'I'm going to Wellington today?'

'That's right.'

'Who's paying for that?'

'The lawyer,' I soothed. The management of his meagre wealth had long been in the hands of a family lawyer.

'He'd better be,' spluttered the uncle. 'Because I haven't got any money.'

A silence. Then: 'So I'm going to Wellington *today*.' This last word was shrill with incredulity.

And as always, he ended as he began: 'I'm sorry, Peter, but I can't make head or tail of this.'

We walked in the gardens for a while and he took my arm. For a moment there was a chilling lucidity.

'You know, Peter,' he said, 'since Joyce died I haven't really enjoyed it much.'

I slopped some more merlot into the tumbler as the men of the family, my cousin and his brother-in-law, beckoned me outside. There in the hallway, in hushed tones, as though it were something of a guilty secret, they told me that Geoff – my uncle, Mum's brother – had left Mum $15,000.

But in death, as in life, Geoff couldn't restrain himself from dispensing to his little sister advice that was indistinguishable from instruction. She was, he had said, to spend the money – more money than she'd seen at any one time in the 30 years since my father had walked out on her – on a trip to England.

Geoff had been on ahead. Busy and curious, he had poked and peered around Cornwall and Yorkshire (the seats, respectively, of his maternal and paternal forebears) and distilled his experiences into two books that recorded the family history. Self-published labours of love, they summarised with an almost actuarial precision, the movements and resting places of the most obscure members of the family. Along the way they paid glancing tribute to some of the more eminent citizens both here and there, as if their very mention might cause some of their nobility to rub off.

Now he wanted Mum to make the same pilgrimage and had left her money for the purpose, so that she might, in her last years, see where it had all started. He wanted her to see their father's birthplace in Leeds and to travel the same roads from Penzance to Plymouth that her maternal great-grandparents, Henry and Priscilla White, had anxiously travelled on their way to board the barque *Westminster* for a small, new country on the other side of the world.

But his instruction was easier to issue than obey. 'We'll see about that,' Mum would say over succeeding months as I harassed her to buy a ticket and go. Her cousin near Leicester, barely an hour north of London by train, welcomed the idea and offered to ferry her around in the north and the south.

It took me longer than it ought to have to realise that she was scared. She had never been further than Australia – a six-day break on the Gold Coast in the 1960s and a Garden Society tour of Tasmania 25 years later. A fussy, fretful octogenarian, less at ease in the world than many of her contemporaries, she found motoring the 200 kilometres to Hamilton to visit old friends an undertaking full of danger and challenge. How could I hope that she would undertake the enormous physical and logistical challenge of a round-the-world flight?

At length I stopped dismissing her unease as the silly fretfulness of an old lady. Heathrow, after all, is intimidating for any traveller; for an elderly woman, limping on a new hip and dazzled by changes in time zones, currencies, customs and accents, it would seem like a fevered nightmare.

So I decided to take her. I would lead her through the hard bits, just as she once led me through the hard bits, holding her steady to stop her falling as she walked through a dangerous world, just as she once did for me.

The mid-afternoon road is empty and I am almost home. Maybe 200 metres separates me from the familiar, predictable order, but it might as well be a million miles.

At the corner ahead, an unsealed dead-end road leads up to

half a dozen farms. The tyres of exiting cars have painted the tarmac into clay-coloured arcs and in the air hangs the dust thrown up by a car that has not long ago pulled away, spitting gravel into the verge of unkempt grass. The houses between me and the corner sit on sections bare of trees and offer no cover higher than a bed of pansies. I can be seen for miles. I begin to run, my leather schoolbag, looped around my shoulders, bouncing off my bum.

The loose stones on the tarseal make the surface uneven and slippery but my pace does not slacken as I pass the road head. Plastic sandals clack. Legs blur.

Then suddenly they are there as if they always have been, materialised by my arrival in their malevolent force field. I pull up, defeated. They are tall, neatly turned out and they wear dress gloves like grown-ups wear.

One is blonde, with ponytails swaying from beneath her maroon bonnet; the other, dark-eyed, has a cruel face and a hooked nose, which, it absurdly occurs to me, might peck my eyes out. They circle on their bikes, far enough away to be able to change direction suddenly if I fancy I see an escape route and make to break. They can stop instantly – touching a levered handbrake and balancing on the polished toe of an improbably tiny shoe – but they are not at rest. They can start again in an instant, heaving their weight aloft on a pedal and cranking the wheels into motion to head me off by simply making a new circle, with the same frightened boy at its centre.

Every so often one swoops and swipes at me, or pinches or grabs a flap of ear roughly between her gloved thumb and fingertip. One flicks the baby-blue sunhat with its Foreign Legion neck flap from my head and it lies on the road; the other rides back and forth over it leaving grubby streaks of tyre and dirt.

'Ooooh, look!' cries one. 'Now his hat's dirty. Mummy *won't* be happy.'

'Who's a *very* bad boy?' says the other.

As they circle they keep up the talk, filling the silence with threatening noise. Their chant is a tormentors' duet, sneering and discordant, a round song in which one always starts before the other finishes. I freeze in the dust and fight back tears. Mostly I don't want to cry because they are girls.

I've grown used to this ritual, which occurs every few days, always at unpredictable intervals. It may be the result more of convenience or coincidence than calculation, but the effect is devastating. Just when I have begun to think they have decided to leave me in peace, they reappear and the shock is like the first time.

Consumed by their taunting presence, I don't notice the car skid to a halt. The avenger is among them before I realise what is happening. It's the car I see first, the elegant sweeping lines of the silver-grey and navy two-tone Daimler Conquest. Its door is open and I can see the walnut dashboard and the blue leather upholstery.

With a start of recognition, I realise it's our car and I turn my attention to the two girls. Mum has dragged them from their bicycles (which topple with an agreeably solid clank) and has them in hand, rough knots of maroon blazer in each clenched fist. From time to time, she lets one go for an instant so she can cuff the other across the side of the head with a free hand. But mostly she just holds on and they don't even struggle to get away.

She is bellowing at them and they cower as she shakes them, promising that they will get 'what for' if they don't leave me alone. They seem to regard this as a disagreeable proposition. They have no idea what 'what for' is, though they reason, soundly enough, that it's a good deal worse than being dragged from your bike and marauded by an angry mother. I notice as they remount and pedal away panic-stricken that their ties are skewed and that old Hook Nose clutches her bonnet, which is crushed by her grip on the handlebars.

Sniffling, I pull myself together as Mum picks up my hat and dusts it off and I clamber into the car's cool interior and collapse against the soft leather of the seat. I ride home in splendour.

A few weeks later, I see the girls for the last time. They are in the distance, riding with a kind of slow, stately dignity, their stockinged knees rising and falling, when they catch sight of me. The effect is electric. The balance of their riding becomes suddenly wobbly and uncertain. One turns hard left onto the verge and the other makes a messy U and begins pedalling back the way she came. Then, after what must have been a brief consultation, they disappear down a public path that leads to the state house subdivision on the other side of the road.

In emotional terms, the trip to England was an undertaking as reckless as it was resonant. Like most men of my age – I was more than halfway through my fiftieth year when we finally got away – I found it hard to be around an often cantankerous and controlling old woman who, like so many women of her age, still hadn't quite accepted that her four sons were out of school uniform. It would be a trial to spend 12 days in the company of someone who usually managed to exhaust my patience in an afternoon.

For her it would be a visit to a place she dimly regarded as home. Like many of her generation, Mum grew up regarding herself less as a New Zealander than as an Englishwoman marooned in an alien land. Without even being fully conscious of the fact, she raised us (on English food) to treasure, as part of our birthright, the bulldog spirit of the Royal Family in the Blitz. We learned to recite John Masefield's *Cargoes* and to excitedly rehearse Nelson's bravura gesture of feigned blindness at Trafalgar or Drake's casual game of bowls on the Hoe at Plymouth as the Spanish Armada approached. I grew up knowing the composition of the Round Table and thrilling to stories of Churchill and Macbeth. It was not until I was in my thirties that I heard of Parihaka or began to read Sargeson. It was later still that I began to look closely at McCahon and realise that his landscapes possessed a hallucinatory clarity that was virtually photographic in its realism.

To take Mum to England would be to take her home to a place she'd never been. But it was also a gesture of respect. I wanted to do it for her. The whole of life is short, they say, but the period between when we start forgiving our parents and when they die is pitilessly so. My father had died – suddenly, sadly and alone – before I even began to love him as a grown-up man should love his father. The last time I spoke to him, three days before he died, I called him a stupid old bugger – a not inaccurate assessment – and hung up on him. With Mum, perhaps, I had the chance to make it different, to make my peace with a woman with whom I had been, for most of my adult life, exasperated and infuriated. Maybe, before she died, I could find out what it was to love her again.

For as long as I can remember, Mum has been a remote figure on the other end of a weekly or fortnightly phone call, with a series of stories about daily life which I struggled to pay attention to. To take her to England would be to resume the relationship we had not had for more than three decades but with the roles reversed.

The trip – assuming that I could persuade her to go through with it – would be an endless series of problems for me to solve. Yet my memory is of her as my problem solver. I grew up astonished at the competence of all adults, and of Mum in particular. The tracks of the old Hornby train set, which twisted and spilt the locomotive even on the easiest corners, were no match for Mum's manipulations of a small pair of pliers. Cowboys' gun belts that needed a new hole pierced or Apache arrows that failed to fly true were quickly and expertly repaired.

'I always wanted to be a wife and a mother,' Mum often said. 'I loved having babies and making a home.' As an adult I struggled to suppress my impatience at this assertion. I'd grown up as part of a generation that entirely distrusted any woman whose ambitions were to be a mother and home-maker. Now we are forced to contemplate the possibility that our palming our own children off into day care from an early age may have given them a burden different from but as heavy as the one we carried. We came from a generation that felt smothered by the attention of mothers who had no life beyond that of their children; our children, perhaps, will come to resent us for leaving them alone too much.

In the 1970s, bolstered by the fiery rhetoric of Germaine Greer, we dismissed contented home-makers as the ignorant stooges of a plot hatched by the patriarchy to keep women in chains. Later, that attitude has softened as I've come to understand that many of our mothers, those women of the post-war generation, might have had other ambitions, but were thwarted by the orthodoxy that required them to breed the workforce that would be the lifeblood of the economic recovery and would pay for the welfare state.

Of course, it's entirely possible that Mum looks back down the years and makes her ambitions rhyme with her achievements. It would be hard to recall a life devoted to raising a family and wistfully remark that it would have been good to be a cartographer, say, or an alpine tour guide.

Certainly Mum never expressed a desire to do anything other than what she did, which was to be at home each day when we left for school and at home when we came back. I used to wonder how she kept busy all that time but, when I stayed home sick from school I saw that she was constantly working, washing and ironing and sewing and baking and bottling and gardening and cleaning and preparing food. Once, when she had dried and put away the last of the lunch dishes she sighed as she passed a tea towel across the already spotless bench and said: 'I suppose I had better start thinking about dinner.' It amazed me. The afternoon stretched, endless and unfillable and dinner seemed as remote a concept as the twenty-first century. But for her it was the next in an endless round of jobs.

And among those jobs, it seemed there was nothing she couldn't do. All my wonder at the ability of adults to make things work was located in my view of her – particularly since my father was incapable of taking on the simplest manual task without destroying something and injuring someone, usually but not always himself.

It may well be that if I'd asked Mum to help me lever a punctured bicycle tyre off the wheel she, too, would have attacked it with gusto and screwdrivers and the tube would have slipped out of its slot with 16 new holes neatly nicked in its powdered rubber. But somehow I doubt it. I never came across a problem Mum couldn't solve, though it was not until years later that I realised she couldn't solve the one problem that truly mattered to her: how to hold on to the man she agreed to marry.

It was, of course, never meant to be easy. Our first plans were derailed early by the collapse of her hip, and the prospect of the trip receded as we negotiated the long process of securing her an elective operation on the crowded public hospital waiting lists. Her convalescence was slow and, although I nagged her to follow a regime of daily walks to prepare for the streets of London, I had only her word that she was ready.

We were initially booked to leave on September 16, 2001 and I admit with some shame that I struggled to see the terrorist attacks on the World Trade Center and the Pentagon as a geopolitical upheaval rather than a personal inconvenience. A year's worth of arrangements went up in smoke. Mother was devastated. Glumly, as we realised that a week's worth of cancelled flights had corroded all the consequential bookings in the UK, she began to unpack everything. The whole enterprise was postponed for a year.

Even then, we nearly didn't make it. My brother called six days before we were due to leave. He'd taken a call from Mum's neighbours, who explained that she had 'had a fall'. She had been taken to hospital for observation, he said, and while it didn't sound serious, I had to face the fact that 'a few small clouds were visible on the horizon'.

Surly, resentful and catastrophising, I bullied my way through rush-hour traffic to the hospital and found her, bristling with exploratory needles, lying mournful in a crudely curtained alcove in the emergency room. She was belligerent about her situation, seeming to construe her confinement as some sort of personal affront.

'I'm perfectly all right,' she insisted, alternating between childish tears and impatience.

She had paused before climbing into the ambulance only long enough to gather up what she referred to as 'my medication' as though it were an old friend. And it was hard to see it as anything else: a two-litre ice-cream container filled with bottles, blister packs and plastic jars. But in the emergency room, the definition of 'my medication' was suddenly contestable. Her list of allowable pharmaceuticals (which would have subdued a small village in the Third World for several months) was suddenly redefined.

I found her reaching for a pathetic quotient of pills that the charge nurse had allowed her. Disgruntled at the disruption, she was swallowing them greedily and rolling her eyeballs as the nurse tried to explain that the decision about what was and was not allowable rested entirely with the doctors.

'No, dear,' she said, mustering a good impression of patience. 'This one is for the heart; I have to have it.'

The fall had been caused by the neighbours' dog, bounding at her in that animated spirit of friendliness that has always seemed to me not easily distinguishable from a savage attack. Standing on her sloping driveway, nattering over the hedge, she had been upended and dropped on her outstretched hand like a spear-tackled league player. The horrified dog owners had taken her inside and patched up her grazes. She had obliged by fainting and they'd called an ambulance.

She was kept in the hospital for three nights as she fulminated and fretted. 'I'm perfectly all right, I tell you!' she kept telling the staff, and later complained to me that 'I keep telling them I'm all right, but they won't listen!' Consultants passed by on their rounds, peered at electrocardiograms, sucked air through their teeth and wondered aloud at the wisdom of travelling.

On the phone, Mum was a touching mixture of tearful vulnerability and ramshackle determination. 'It's going to take more than this to keep me down,' she said, her voice trembling. 'I've told them I'm going and that's that.'

That was that, as it happened. Discharged barely 72 hours before we were due to leave, she was triumphant. I began my packing, too, though with a heavy heart, somehow certain that something would go wrong.

If I was in any doubt about what I was taking on, my brothers and friends lost no time in dispelling it. The plan was madness, they cried with one voice. They knew how difficult she could be. So did I. In her later middle age and now, on the verge of dotage, Mum had often been fretful and difficult.

Certainly I was not beyond thinking that some sort of guilt drove what I was doing. Mum was nearing the end of a lifetime of self-denial and disappointment and it seemed worth giving her some happy memories to take to the grave.

But there was more than pity at work here. I wanted to do it for myself, too. Taking her along gave a solid sense of purpose to my trip. And I hoped I might learn something about myself. I sensed that a return to her roots, to my roots, might offer a chance to take stock, to get a deeper sense of being not an Englishman manqué but a native of another country.

This, then, is her story. But, very probably, in ways I don't yet fully understand, it's mine, too.

PACIFIC CLASS

Mum's on the phone. She can't find her passport.

'You haven't got it, have you?' she asks tremulously.

'Why would I have it?'

'I don't know,' she grumbles. 'I thought perhaps I'd given it to you to buy the ticket or something. I'm blowed if I can find it.'

She's been packing for weeks, rehearsing a procedure she had already perfected a year before. Each day she frets and folds and tucks, bending over suitcases at the foot of her bed. Each time she finds new, clever places to stow small items, which she is then unable to find.

She rings back an hour later, triumphant.

'I've found it!' she says. 'It was in the front pocket all along, but I'd put it inside the brown wallet.'

Meanwhile, she showers me with correspondence: letters containing lists of her medication or all her traveller's cheque numbers for me to carry as backups. Another letter records that she has had a visit from the local vicar.

'I have put him au fait with everything,' she says, adding ominously that 'everything' includes 'getting permission to use the church for my funeral'.

'You will be pleased to know,' she writes, 'that as a result of his visit and prayers, all my anxiety has gone and I am confident that I will get through this trip with the Lord's protection. So now all my bases are covered and I can relax.'

The letter is dated exactly three weeks before we are due to leave, and I wish I could relax. I am having trouble reconciling the excitement I always feel about travelling with a creeping sense of doom that something will go terribly wrong.

I go to visit her and am pleasantly surprised by the economy of her packing. She has filled two cases – one medium, one small cabin-size – with her belongings, carefully choosing, and where necessary borrowing, miniature versions of everyday items like her radio. I ferret through the case, removing stuff that

I will have – a first-aid kit, for example, and a torch.

'What!' she wails. 'I'll need that when I go up to Cousin David's!'

'I'm sure he'll have a torch,' I say. I tell her to put it away, although I have no doubt it will find its way back into the case the moment I leave.

Once, of course, she packed for me, tucking lovingly into corners small tokens of home, like a lunchbox filled with home-made biscuits. Their function varied according to the moment and my need: talismans against homesickness or barter material for midnight feasts. On the underside of the lid of a tartan family suitcase, stuck in place with tape that had turned fly-paper-gooey with age, was a list of what had to go in the case. It was a checklist for me, to make sure that I brought back everything I'd taken, but Mum's handsome cursive handwriting was a kind of anchor chain for me, too, a link with home.

The rest of my packing was full of her handiwork, too, including, on one church camp, a home-made sleeping bag – blankets hand sewn together and covered with faded curtaining.

I stand back and survey the big bag before trying to close the lid. The jaws meet with a satisfyingly easy click.

'That's good, Mum,' I say. 'You've done well.'

'Thank you, dear,' she says. 'You're looking after everything.'

Being looked after is not part of Mum's emotional landscape. Not since she came upon the lifeless form of her father near the gate leading to the orchard in their home in Papatoetoe.

She was only four-and-a-half, too young to be fatherless. She embraced the body that lay on the ground near the gate, willing it to wake. The morning air was full of the rasp of crickets, and incurious bees grazed the furry clover flowers. More than 80 years stretched before her then. Robbed of the most important man in her life, she would mourn for maleness. As an adult, she would be surrounded by four sons. She would lose, at less than two days old, the daughter who might have made things better.

Later, much later, her brother would write of his father's death that 'suicide was never considered seriously as a possibility': 'It was judged that [he] had been disturbed by yowling cats, a continuing nuisance to us, as he tried unsuccessfully to sleep – a difficulty he faced a great deal.'

That single sentence is plump with unanswered questions. As I grew up, I was often quick to hiss from open windows at cats engaged in aggressive stand-offs, which filled the night air with their whining growls. I enjoyed the thrill of fear as I threw the window open and came so close to the raw, animal sound; but more, I enjoyed the sense of power, the knowledge that I could send the unseen opponents scurrying explosively in opposite directions. What need did I have for a .22 to send them packing? My guns – which in any case were far more fearsome, .45 calibre revolvers at least – were imaginary appliances, made to police the wild, wide range of the back lawn or the paddocks beyond, which went on as far as Morrinsville.

In any case, beyond the 'nuisance' of the cats lies a more suggestive phrase: he had 'great difficulty' sleeping.

'So it seemed,' Geoff continues, 'that, distressed by sleeplessness, he took his rifle to attempt to frighten the cats away; perhaps he thought he might even hit one. But how he would believe he could shoot accurately in the dark can only indicate his distress.'

A few lines later, the noose of explanation tightens, although there's no indication that Geoff knows he's tugging it tighter with every word.

'Dad,' he writes, 'had experienced trouble with "nerves" … and he had great difficulty in sleeping. I can remember him using a battery-operated therapy for which he held an electrode in each hand to receive a mild, pulsating electric shock, supposed then to be helpful for such nervous disorders. I suspect he had an anxiety neurosis.'

The diagnosis is more than suggestive. A man who can't sleep, so riven by anxiety that he resorts to an appliance that sounds like it comes from the catalogue of a snake-oil salesman but which was, perhaps, a form of electro-convulsive therapy, goes cat-hunting in the pre-dawn gloom. He may have been a particularly bad shot but how he managed to train the gun on himself is a matter Mum and her brother were forbidden – or forbade themselves – to contemplate.

When I was growing up, people seemed frequently and inordinately careless about climbing through fences and, for all I know, about climbing trees as well. They always seemed to do so with loaded guns, and the guns always seemed to be cocked and on a hair trigger. I always wondered how they managed it, how a strand of tautly stretched number 8 wire could snake its way around the trigger of a 12-gauge, which was, as any trigger-happy backyard cowboy knew, encircled by a solid trigger guard.

The stories of these tragic deaths – one was of a teacher at my school – were often told in hushed conclaves of adults in corners of rooms. 'What is happening?' we would ask, and the adults would disperse as they suddenly discovered some task that required their urgent attention. They plainly knew what for us was a chilling, inchoate suspicion, but it was not until years later that the truth dawned on me: the wire was part not just of a fence but of a web of soothing euphemism. It was easier for all of us to accept that the callous hand of fate had dealt a death blow than to contemplate the unthinkable – that a man had headed off into the great New Zealand outdoors, there to rest against a tree and prop the muzzle of a gun in his mouth.

Disguising the dark truth was in tune with the prevailing wisdom of the years in which I grew up. We lived in a land of plenty, brightly lit by the optimism of a world war won. We did not care to make room for stories laced with despair, about men who didn't have the heart to sit at a table so laden with good fortune, who turned their backs on life.

Certainly Mum is in no doubt now that Frank died by his own hand. She did not, as we grew up thinking, discover him dead.

'I climbed out of my cot and went into the kitchen,' she recalls. 'I knew something was wrong because the kettle was boiling its head off on the primus stove. I went outside and by the time I got there he was laid out and they'd cleaned him up a bit, but there was one clean hole in the middle of his forehead and looking back I realise that it was no accident.'

It was the last she saw of her father, she says. Kids weren't allowed to go to the funeral.

Mum's mother – her name was the delightfully antique Adeline Priscilla, but we called her Nana – was the only grandparent I knew, since Dad's parents were both dead before I turned two. I remember her as a dour and unsmiling figure whose very presence seemed to chide us for our complacency, bathed as we were in post-war plenty, though Mum assures me she never smiled because she felt unwelcome in my father's presence.

Sometimes we would pick her up after we had been to church (she never came, we were told, because church made her cry by reminding her of her wedding and Frank's funeral) and take her home for Sunday lunch. En route from car to kitchen, her gaze would alight on a couple of wayward weeds in a flower bed and, all got up in her best frock, her purse hooked over the crook of her arm, she would place a sensibly low-heeled shoe in a space among the plants and bend to the task someone else had missed.

Mum's abiding memory of her mother is of a woman on her knees, which seems apt. Nana's early widowhood – she was a few weeks shy of her thirty-ninth birthday when Frank shot himself on October 13, 1925 – condemned her to a life of unremitting toil. Unable to support the family on a meagre widow's pension, she rented a house in Ranfurly Road in Epsom and turned the only skill she had – keeping house – into a money-making proposition by taking in boarders.

'She just got on with it,' Mum recalls. 'She had to make a living and provide for two children. But every time I came home she was on her knees, in the garden perhaps, or polishing the kitchen floor. I caught her once polishing the floor and crying her heart out.'

When Nana died, 50 years after Frank, she left among her belongings a note that finished with the words: '… I have never deserved the punishment I have suffered over all the years through no fault of mine.'

The first time I heard this, it chilled me. It seemed such a cruel legacy, a ringing reproof to the children she knew would find it as they sorted through her belongings.

But it rang a bell for me, too, of days when I would return from school to find Mum hard at work. She would not be on hands and knees exactly, but knee-deep in laundry in the age just before automatic washing machines. And I could tell she'd been crying.

I longed, with the intense determination only a small boy can have, to rescue her, even though I dimly sensed that I was part of the reason for her imprisonment.

The inflight services director materialises by my seat. It seems like the early hours, because I have just woken and in the darkened cabin everyone is asleep around me. I make my dry and sticky eyes gape, trying to bring the face of my watch and my mind into focus. In New Zealand it is dawn, which means that where we are it is the day before we left.

'We've had a bit of a problem with your mum,' he says unsmilingly. My heart drops. I have visions of a cardiac incident, a massive thrombosis, a premature apocalyptic attack of homesickness.

The reality is far more prosaic. Inexplicably, given her limited mobility, they have seated her in the upstairs business class cabin, which is far enough from my seat in economy class for me to disclaim her if the going gets really rough. And, I figured, by paying a business class fare she has bought the right to be a bit of extra bother.

But no money bought this. Her mind fevered by dire newspaper warnings about deep vein thrombosis, she has been dragging herself to her feet every few minutes all night and pacing the wide aisles. The thought of an orthopaedically compromised octogenarian lurching up and down the darkened business class aisle, brushing against sleeping elbows and ankles, is terrifying enough. Travellers up the front of the aircraft expect to be among their own kind, not saddled with nervous, novice flyers.

But it is worse. She has, it transpires, been hauling her not inconsiderable bulk to its feet using the seat-back of the poor individual in front of her; on occasion she has apparently grabbed fistfuls of his hair, which, it turns out, is the luxuriant, brilliantined kind that typically belongs to Mediterranean types with short fuses.

The genial Maori steward who is in charge of our section of economy class flashes me a smile. He has been good to me all night, not, I suspect, because he likes the cut of my jib, but because I am sitting next to two Maori boys who are heading off to separate rugby engagements – one as a coach, one as a player – in different parts of the UK. He has plied us with the oversupply of tasty desserts from the business class section and now he is plying me with encouragement.

'Hasn't he got a mother, bro?' he asks me rhetorically later when no one is listening. 'We've all got mothers. They looked after us and now it's our turn to look after them.'

I feel like hugging him, but the director of operations is dealing with matters with the precision and correctness befitting his position.

'He's not happy,' he says, referring to the Spaniard. His expression suggests he is attempting a diplomatic understatement. 'He's talking about compensation from the airline and all the rest of it.'

Unwilling to contemplate, much less ask, what 'all the rest of it' might be, I eye the staircase behind him. He moves, almost imperceptibly, to block my path.

'I don't want you going up there till the morning,' he says. 'It will just disturb people more.'

High above the Pacific, as the aircraft crosses the international dateline, I begin, not for the first time, to have serious doubts about the entire undertaking.

In the end, they shunt the much-abused Spaniard up to first class. 'That'll shut him up,' they say.

When we land in Los Angeles I brace myself for the protestations of innocence from my mother. But she seems sublimely indifferent, if not oblivious, to the mayhem she has caused.

Los Angeles is still, a year later, in the grip of 9/11 fever. The old transit lounges, which allowed passengers passing through to be excused the indignity of immigration, are gone. The Americans plainly don't want anyone on their soil, even for a couple of hours, that they haven't had a chance to eyeball. So the 747 disgorges its passengers, dazed by changes of time zone, into long queues that snake through geometric mazes of tape-and-post aisles. It is here that I learn the magic that resides in the words 'wheelchair service'.

He is there, standing at the end of the air-bridge by the aircraft door, when we emerge. An ancient Filipino, he tells me his name is Nicolas and points to his laminated identity card to confirm the fact. It strikes me, as he shepherds us through immigration and security checks, that he is barely younger than the woman he is pushing; but he is lean and fit, and still hard at work. Age has not wearied him and he moves through the bustle as though being paid a bonus for speed.

He is familiar, too, with the needs of the long-distance flier: as we emerge from the immigration hall into the terminal proper he points me to the concourse outside.

'You wanna smoke?' he asks, holding up two fingers and miming a cigarette into his mouth.

'You betcha!' I reply, shuddering at the thought of the shuffling queues we have left behind, and I pull out my tobacco.

'So, Mum, here we are,' I say, as I roll up. 'This is LA.'

'Doesn't look like much to me,' she harrumphs.

I have to admit she has a point. Terminal entrances are never the most impressive of places. This is like every other day I have stepped out of the cool terminal interior and crossed the boundary from airport to America. Taxis and limos and shuttle buses and rental car companies' courtesy vehicles pull up or pull away in a constant roaring procession. Beyond, the City of Angels slumps in the heat, plaster and tile under an orange blanket of smog. I try to imagine a world beyond airports and arrangements and anxieties but it won't come into focus.

As I smoke, Mum tries to engage Nicolas in conversation.

'Haven't you retired yet?' she asks, a tad accusingly I think. Then, perhaps sensing the possibility of being misinterpreted, she adds, 'I don't know how you do it.' And to me, 'It's marvellous, really, what they do.'

When we reach the calm and cool of the club lounge, I realise to my horror that I am in the land of the tip without any American currency. I spread my empty wallet in front of Nicolas' eyes and he tries to turn them away. Suddenly I remember the New Zealand $5 note in my shirt pocket and pass it to him. Without a word, a sound, or even a facial expression, he makes it leave my hand and disappear into his pocket. For a moment I picture his horror when he finds out it is less than half its face value in the land of the free and the home of the brave. But my anxiety eases when I realise later that, as an Air New Zealand employee, permanently assigned to ferrying demanding and disabled New Zealanders about, he would be used to a tight-fistedness that is deliberate rather than forgetful, a cultural practice rather than a lapse of memory.

'I'll come and get you when it's time to board,' he says (to Mum rather than me). 'Don't go anywhere.'

Mum, choosing an armchair in the middle of the room to maximise her audibility, wonders loudly what to do next.

'I'm not sure whether to go to the toilet or have my pills,' she bellows as I pile our cabin bags beside the chair.

'Well, whatever you do,' I reply in an urgent stage whisper, 'I am sure the rest of the room doesn't need to be included in your decision-making.' I wrestle with the urge to crash-tackle her into the seat.

'Don't be so silly,' she splutters. 'Nobody wants to listen to me.'

'My point exactly,' I say, under my breath.

'What?'

'Nothing.'

I head for the shower, which is full; so I decide to make the most of the wait by checking with the lounge staff to see if Mum can be shifted from the upstairs cabin so I can keep a closer eye on her.

I take Mum's passport and boarding pass, both of which I have sole charge of, over to the desk and explain the situation. The woman behind the counter looks puzzled, even sceptical.

'If you check with the cabin crew,' I am tempted to say, 'I think you'll find they would welcome the idea.'

The woman's American accent and contained, courtly manner somehow don't match her Air New Zealand livery. New Zealanders abroad welcome dealing with New Zealanders for their cheerfully gruff and businesslike manner. There can be nothing more welcome to a Kiwi traveller with a problem than the ethnically Kiwi hometown answer: 'No [which means yes], that's no problem.' At a pinch, an Australian 'No worries' will do, but there's nothing like the local lilt.

This American in Kiwi uniform seems to know what she is doing, though, so I turn away. Mum is now surrounded by several men, prostrate in a fair imitation of the Muslim prayer position.

'Here's one,' bellows one of them, rising to his knees and inspecting a pill between thumb and forefinger.

'Oh, thank you,' Mum is saying. 'That's almost all of them now. The bottle top's so tight. It's a fool of a thing.'

Shuddering I go for a shower. When I emerge a few minutes later I am feeling clean and refreshed, but I break into an instant cold sweat at what I see. The Air New Zealand woman is leaning over Mum, who gazes up from her armchair, nodding in the peculiarly rhythmical way that people do when they haven't the faintest idea what's going on. I bustle over.

'I was just telling your mother,' she says as I approach, 'that we *can* move her, but I won't get the seat allocation for … '

'Thanks a lot,' I say, trying to bring the conversation to a hasty end. But it is too late.

'How did you come by my passport?' Mum is demanding. Heads swivel nearby and the airline woman turns to me. Gulping like a beached fish, she is trying to speak, but no words are coming out. I know how she feels.

'Thanks a lot,' I repeat, almost shoving her in the direction of the counter. 'I'll take it from here.'

At the bank of phones nearby, a man of Middle Eastern extraction is talking to his son just slightly louder than necessary, as people always do on international calls, and loud enough to be clearly audible to us. Oddly, he is speaking not in his native tongue, but in a heavily accented English. The reason for his choice of language soon becomes clear.

'Be good boy,' he is saying, 'and practise your English.'

I become aware of a cooing sound to my right and look up to see that it is emerging from Mum, who is making the kind of noise an eight-year-old girl makes when she sights a week-old, wet-eared puppy.

'Oh, look,' she says, drawing the last word out so long it sounds like a singer's vocal-cord-stretching exercise. 'He's talking to his boy.' I flinch and hunch lower in the seat as she adds 'in Arabia', doubtless believing that to be the name of a country.

I bury my nose in the *Los Angeles Times* as she opines at immoderate volume that he is 'such a lovely father'. This is an improvement on 'They are such lovely fathers', which is the style of her normal back-handed compliment to dark races, as though such things as kindly parenting are the sole preserve of Europeans.

I can see her brow crinkle as she begins to assemble a speech of congratulations about how sweet he is ('You really are very loving, you people, aren't you?') to be delivered as soon as he hangs up and I hastily concentrate all my mental energy, like a hypnotist, into stopping her. It works. By the time he rings off she is wondering aloud where she's put her passport.

'I have it,' I say.

Before long, Nicolas reappears. The derisory tip has not been enough to frighten him off, apparentl, though I guess he still has time to stop suddenly and pitch Mum down a flight of stairs. For a moment an unworthy thought crosses my mind, but soon we are at the gate lounge and the ground staff are telling me I have been upgraded to business class.

Welcome though this news is, I waste no time imagining that it is a perk for me. More probably I am being sworn in as a deputy cabin attendant, with special responsibility for the elderly woman in 9J. But in fact they've moved her downstairs, and I have the best upgrade of all – I am also now in the downstairs section of business class, but 'Unfortunately we haven't been able to seat you and your mum together.'

As I make my way to my place, I tell Mum's new seatmate,

who has a window spot, that I am willing to swap if he wants.

'Let's see how we go,' he says gaily, plainly oblivious to what he is in for. I look back at him during the flight a few times. Each time Mum is talking and he is nodding, his eyes glaze. I signal to the cabin staff for another glass of a particularly toothsome chablis.

Beside me is an old man who turns out to be an elderly and apparently prosperous Lithuanian Jew who lives in New York. For a few minutes I find him interesting, until I realise that his arrogance expresses itself in speaking too softly to be audible. He persists in the habit as the hosties try to make sense of his food and drink orders, leaning forwards the better to hear. He drops things too often for it to be accidental, and I realise that he is enjoying the semblance of obeisance this pantomime creates, not to mention the chance to peer down the front of the hosties' dresses. Perhaps, I begin to think, the woman formerly seated in 9J is not the worst passenger one might have charge of.

At last we are there, plunging through the maelstrom and being pitched out into the concourse. Crowds of people awaiting their loved ones' arrival form a horseshoe behind waist-high fences. Beyond is a line of drivers with the names of the people they are meant to be picking up felt-tipped onto plastic paddles, which they hold at chest height. I scan them with no great hope that our name will be among them. It isn't.

Waves of tiredness have been wrestling for several hours now with an almost boyish sense of excitement. I am longing to prop myself on the right side of a pint of bitter and watch as the city's distinctive black cabs nose through narrow streets. Now I have to fight off frustration as well. Breathing deeply I go to a newsagent's, buy a phone card and call the driver's mobile phone number.

It turns out he is tied up with an American couple who were halfway to Heathrow, where he was due to drop them off and pick us up, before they told him they were flying out of Gatwick. Even on a quiet Sunday he is many long minutes away, and since he has the key to our apartment, we have no choice but to wait for him.

I haul Mum and the bags over to a waiting area away from

the press of people and we try to rest. I scan the middle distance anxiously searching for a bar or café, although I know it is hopeless. Apart from a newsagent's, this echoing hall seems to be nothing more than a tail race down which people pour into the country. Even if I could see one, leaving Mum alone in such a thief-friendly environment as a crowded arrivals hall is scarcely the act of a good shepherd.

John, the driver, arrives soon enough, flustered and apologetic. 'Bloody Yanks,' he concludes, shaking his head. Evidently he assumes a shared and implicitly anti-American cultural heritage and has decided that appealing to our baser instincts is the way to smooth the feathers ruffled by our wait. In fact, we are not upset. A certain resignation creeps into the long-haul flyer's view of the world. The entire undertaking is such a nightmare that anything short of actual physical assault is treated as part of the game. But we are glad to see him.

He helps us drag our baggage to his waiting car, which turns out to be one of the new 'black cabs', the commonest vehicles on London streets. In fact, it isn't black, though many are; his is maroon and the doors have been sold to some commercial sponsor. What's more, the interior coachwork is much more utilitarian, even bus-like, than evocative. A small sign on each door proclaims that it is auto-locked while the cab is moving (doing a runner at the lights, or even when the car is in slow motion in busy traffic, must be a popular pursuit and a cabbie's occupational hazard). Another sign, above the window behind the driver's shoulder, advises that 'When the red light is on, the driver may be able to hear what you are saying.' I like that 'may be able to', which carries at once the suggestion that he will only answer your stupid questions if he feels inclined and the warning that anything you say might be overheard.

As he loads the bags in, I take Mum in search of a ladies' room. Two policemen pass, not the high-helmeted ''allo, 'allo, 'allo', hands-behind-back bobbies of popular image but flak jacketed and watchful, holding semi-automatic weapons diagonally across their chests with their fingers lying flat alongside the trigger guards. I catch the eye of one of them and flash him a smile that is intended to be friendly. He assesses me unsmilingly for a second and his look moves on.

The cab barrels along strangely deserted Sunday morning streets, through Middlesex and into the city, though it is not until we reach Kensington and the Brompton Road that I begin to recognise the street names and have some sense of where we are. The last (and first) time I arrived in London, I crept into the city on the tube. It is good to ride at street level, straining through waves of tiredness to make sense of the passing urban landscape. I wave a hand airily in the direction of Knightsbridge.

'Harrods is up there!' I announce. 'I'll take you there. You'll like that.'

'No, thank you,' Mum harrumphs, her voice heavy with contempt.

'What do you mean, "No, thank you"? I ask.

'Pig of a man, that Al Fayed! I wouldn't darken his door.'

I want her to be more excited than she apparently is. In an instant I am transported back to those times as a small boy when, bursting with excitement, I would tell her about something I had achieved and she, distracted by her private thoughts, would affect an interest she transparently did not feel. I struggle not to be crestfallen and to remind myself that if I am practically hallucinating from tiredness, she is probably feeling a good deal worse.

A lot more quickly than I had expected (we are, after all, paying £40 or almost $130 for the 40-minute cab ride) we reach the apartment in Soho. The good news is that we have the top-floor apartment, which has its own access to a secluded roof garden; the bad news is that the creaky elevator, which barely has room enough for four standing humans, goes only as far as the penultimate floor. As Mum drags her weary bones the last two dozen stairs to apartment 7, I shunt the bags up in relays and wonder, not for the first time, about the wisdom of bringing a guitar.

Before I even make a move to unpack, I duck down to a convenience store on Oxford Street and pick up a bottle of tonic, cadging a paper cup full of ice from the bar on the corner on the way back. Pulling out the duty-free gin, I fix us a large pair of gin and tonics.

'Well, Mum,' I say as we clink glasses on the terrace while the sun glints off the rooftops of Soho, 'we made it.'

She doesn't hear me. She is worrying about where she's put her passport.

MODERN GREEK

Mother has lost 12 hours and can't stop looking for them. Just as she packed and unpacked and repacked her bag before she left, she keeps returning to the issue of what time it is. We left, she remembers, at night and now it's morning. 'That seemed like a very long night,' she says. She can't get used to the idea that time has simultaneously moved forwards and backwards. Patiently I explain – to myself as much as to her – that it may be Sunday morning here but it's Sunday evening in New Zealand. More than a day has passed since we clambered on the aeroplane.

Our apartment in Soho Square is almost directly above the Tottenham Court Road tube station and at the top of Greek Street. It's extraordinary how resonant these names are to me. I dimly remember a character in a cheap novel asking a taxi driver to take him to 'Greek Street, Soho'. It sounded so foreign, it might have been Patagonia or Mongolia. Now here, I find it still exotic but, oddly, reassuringly familiar, too. It is almost as if I have come home.

So close to the bustle and sleazy grime of Oxford Street, the square is a leafy retreat, as quiet and calm as one might expect to find in a small provincial town. On weekdays it fills with lunchtime loungers, who take their shoes off and enjoy the air around the plane trees. These trees, I will later learn, are ideally suited to the grimy urban environment because they absorb the soot-laden air and expel the toxins by continuously shedding their thick bark.

We are so centrally located, I am champing at the bit to hit the streets and enjoy the environment. But Mum's cousin and his wife are due at any moment and there is unpacking and showering to be done. I spend the time rearranging the furniture – the foldaway bed is in Mum's room and modesty demands I drag it along the hall to the lounge. As she fusses in the bathroom, I wrestle with the upended sofa, walking it along the hall and struggling not to shred its already torn fabric on the door runners. The relatives arrive early, looking cool and calm, to find me wrapped in a sarong, sweating profusely and feeling vulgarly colonial.

David thrusts out a hand with a cheery hello. 'Er, yeah, gidday,' I reply.

David Demaine, Mum's cousin, and his wife Margaret are unflappable folk – they'll have to be since they are taking Mum for four weeks after I've finished dragging her around the West Country. They perch on the sofa, politely accepting the G&Ts I pour for them and enthusing about our trip and arrival.

We wander down Greek Street for a bite and settle on a pasta café that looks promising but makes lasagne to the same recipe as the folk who make the frozen 'pasta bakes' advertised on television. It's hideously expensive – three small plates of pasta, a Caesar salad and a couple of glasses of wine set us back more than $100, although when I complain to the waiter who takes our money that a Caesar salad calls for delicately separated whole leaves of cos lettuce and not the roughly hand-shredded outer leaves of an iceberg, he quickly forgoes charging me for it.

Greek Street, they say, gets its name from the Greek Christians fleeing persecution by the Ottomans, who settled here in the late seventeenth century. But there are few Greek restaurants here now. The place is full of the trendiest eateries with prices to match. The most famous is probably The Gay Hussar, notoriously a haunt of the Labour Left – a group now studied by archaeologists rather than political scientists. But it's almost impossible to get a table; they only take bookings a week in advance and if you ring much after 10 a.m. – as I did – the entire following week is full.

Greek Street was also allegedly where Casanova spent a short time in London in 1764 and Thomas de Quincey, the famous English opium eater, proved that dope doesn't have to sap your creativity.

We are in a part of London that has long been home to writers whose names are legendary to me. At the foot of Greek Street is the pub called the Coach and Horses, where Jeffrey Bernard did much, if not most, of the drinking that would kill him. The reliably reprobate columnist for the right-wing but elegantly written magazine *The Spectator*, he was always something of a legend among the more enthusiastically dipsomaniac members of a profession far more bibulous then than now. His column, entitled *Low Life*, was once described admiringly as 'a suicide note in weekly instalments'.

'There is far too much nonsense written about alcohol abuse,' he opined in a typical piece, 'but nobody seems to give a damn about the abuse of alcoholics. Successive governments have wantonly thrown people onto the streets at 3 p.m. and 11 p.m. daily and the Sunday hours are quite simply sadistic and stupid, too. Britain is rapidly becoming a no-smoking area. Sexual intercourse is finished thanks to a drunken sailor and a Haitian pig and there is a licensed drought for 14½ hours every day. For six of those hours I sleep – not easily, I can tell you – and I work, or at least think about it, for the odd half hour. That leaves six hours in which to shave and make a cup of tea. Contemplation of the situation has decided me to go off to look for somewhere to die, as I believe elephants do when life gets them down.'

Bernard's column occasionally failed to appear when his excesses – he invariably referred to his binges as 'appalling behaviour' although there seemed not a trace of remorse or apology in the phrase – got in the way of his deadlines. On those occasions, under the single-column *Low Life* rubric would appear, in italics and without elaboration, the four words 'Jeffrey Bernard is unwell.'

It became his signature phrase, an announcement which, when published, was not an excuse for a column having failed to appear but rather a proclamation of the piece's *raison d'être* – a sort of column in itself.

Jeffrey Bernard ceased being unwell on September 4, 1997. His death followed his decision to withdraw from kidney dialysis because it prevented him from smoking. 'If I believed in life after death,' he had once written, 'I would say there must be a hell of a party going on somewhere.' He deserved to find it.

It's a Sunday, the only Sunday we will spend in London, and

Mum's keen to hear a sung evensong. Strung out by jet lag, I find the idea of sitting in a church, no matter how sublime the singing, slightly horrifying. But it will be our only chance and we battle off through the cluster of streets north of Oxford looking for All Saints in Margaret Street where, we have been told, they take choral music seriously.

At St Aidan's, blond brick and quite devoid of history, they took choral music very seriously indeed. Dad was the choirmaster and the organist, too, though his keyboard skills had never been the same since he neatly removed the end of his thumb with a circular saw.

He'd always fancied himself as something of a handyman, Dad. He returned from town most Friday nights with a new tool – a plane, perhaps, or a drill press, something expensive, made in England or Germany, something that belongs in the workshop of a craftsman. He took his new purchase to a place called 'the shed'. This was a space under the garage where no one could ever find anything, and there Dad would stand, surveying benches covered with broken fretsaw blades or old instant coffee jars of nails with the word 'nails' written boldly on the lid even though the contents are plainly visible through the glass. He would hold his new purchase aloft and look around for a place to hang it before giving up with a sigh and laying it on the bench. There it would be found, years later, still in its paper bag, the 'cash sale' docket precisely quantifying the purchase's futility.

None of us can remember anything he made, though we remember the grumbles of tradesmen he would summon to repair and rehang sticky doors he had butchered by cross-grain planing. My brothers and I knew the shed simply as a fine and private place where Dad was to be left alone; it was not until years later that I realised he spent long afternoons there so he could drink in peace.

As children we cleared a space on the bench to create something. This was usually some form of weapon to destroy some ethnic minority – native Americans, whom we called Injuns, were the most popular – that was resisting the civilising effect of a colonial advance. At the crucial moment Dad materialised beside us to advise us that there was 'a bit of a knack' to a particular procedure we were about to undertake. He offered to show us how it was done (which meant he would do it) and we protested feebly before realising that there was more fun to be had by standing back and watching. There was a sense of inevitability about the way he carefully drilled a hole, selected a screw and attached the crosspiece to a home-made sword, meanwhile attaching the whole weapon – and the end of his tie – to the workbench.

Most of the time, though, he contented himself with the pride of ownership of a tool and was untroubled by the urge to use it. The exception was the circular saw, which he used to slice up pieces of wood for no apparent reason. Perhaps the slicing alone satisfied some sort of atavistic urge to control the world about him or just provided a chance to demonstrate that he had mastery of the requisite knack. Certainly the high, freewheeling whine, dropping in pitch as it bit into timber, was the soundtrack of weekend afternoons.

On one afternoon, the pitch dropped, then rose again accompanied by an explosive 'Shit!'. I ran to the shed and, as my eyes accustomed to the dim light seeping through cobweb-laced windows, I became aware of Dad lying on his back clasping his left thumb between the fingers of his right hand. The initial impression that he had dropped dead was dispelled by the realisation that fresh smoke was rising from the soggy cigarette between his lips. He had, it transpired, adopted his version of the recovery position and I was dispatched to summon help.

Like most comedy, it contains a kernel of tragedy. The upshot was a flat piece of scar tissue on the end of his left thumb which would curse him with a permanent insensitivity and condemn him to playing the cracks between notes on the keyboards of the St Aidan's organ.

The injury alone would pose an obstacle to the technical proficiency he must have aspired to, but his short legs, which could barely reach the organ's foot pedals, added to the difficulty. He had to slide his arse forwards to punch the pedals with the crêpe soles of his corduroy shoes; but from that organist's bench he ruled the choir stalls with an iron determination to make a jumble of housewives and middle managers from insurance firms into a halfway-decent ensemble. He insisted on attendance at weekly choir practices and devised ambitious choral programmes – a weekly anthem, small oratorios or cantatas at Easter or Christmas. And Mum's dramatic contralto was his solid-gold asset.

It was Mum's voice that Dad fell in love with first, and the glimmerings of that love began at a distance long before he heard it. His father, Jasper, would write to him when he was in Egypt during the war, singing the praises of the young contralto in the choir at the Church of the Epiphany where Jasper was the pastor.

He could not have overstated the case. I grew up proud of my mother's singing voice, which I knew instinctively to be a thing of beauty even if I didn't always like the music it produced. Like any youngster, I suppose, I would cringe at the showy descants with which she would sometimes decorate the last verses of big carols in the church choir. But equally I remember listening to her sing on the radio, in sessions recorded at the Hamilton studios of what was then called the NZBC.

Once, we visited the Waitomo Caves, and in the acoustically blessed cave they call the Cathedral, the guide issued an invitation for someone to sing. We knew Mum would and she did, filling the chamber with what I recall as *Drink to Me Only with Thine Eyes* (she says it was *Ave, Maria*). I remember less clearly what she sang than the expressions on the faces of those listening, transfixed by the rich and haunting beauty of her voice.

It was in the autumn of 1944 that the Church of the Epiphany choir was invited to sing at the Harvest Festival at distant Alfriston, Mum recalls.

'That was the time I first really noticed that he was noticing me,' she says. 'I sat on his knee all the way home because there wasn't enough room in the car.'

Later the 22-year-old, by her own admission 'as green as grass', would visit Dad's parents' house in Park Road, Grafton, near the hospital. Dad would play the piano and Mum would sing, as often as not for their own enjoyment as for the entertainment of others. It was a Rachmaninov song called *At Night* that 'did the trick', Mum says.

'It's a beautiful piece and I really let myself go, and when I'd finished he jumped up from the piano and kissed me. It was pretty well all go from there on. He decided he wanted to marry me.'

All Saints is wrapped around scaffolding, which seems to hold up its gloomy vaulted interior. The organ is under repair and atop the scaffolding on painters' planks sit large speakers that will carry the sound of an electronic keyboard.

The speakers amplify the words of the sermon, but do not make them any more intelligible. The preacher is a Korean native who has tried and failed to learn English somewhere in North America. He beams with pride at the elegant construction of his homily, but no one in the congregation has the faintest idea what he is talking about. Making matters worse, I fall asleep suddenly, deeply and repeatedly, and Mum, who seems to be weathering the jet lag a good deal better than I am, has to nudge me awake when I emit a strangled snore.

The choir is good, though, singing Stainer's *Magnificat* and *Nunc Dimittis*. We sit on hard wicker chairs that are joined by battens across their back legs into groups of four. The choristers outnumber the congregation two to one, and the whole procedure is so High Church that we barely recognise it as Anglican. The celebrant priests bow low to each other and swing censers that puff acrid clouds of scented smoke heavenwards. Before long we can barely breathe and we flee for the relatively clean air on the street outside.

David and Margaret see us back to the flat before retreating up north. We sleep the heavy sleep of the geographically disjointed.

I was never much of a tourist. The last (and first) time I went to London, I saw none of the tourist attractions. For five days I luxuriated in the broadsheet papers, finishing breakfast just in time for lunch. I took a boat down the river to Greenwich to the Royal Observatory. Having just read Dava Sobel's *Longitude*, I was keen to see Harrison's clocks, those heroic triumphs of perseverance and ingenuity which had made the greatest contribution since the sextant to accurate navigation. A long-time Shakespeare devotee, I marvelled at a production of *As You Like It* at the reconstructed Globe in Southwark, barely noticing the hard seats and feeling a keen sadness when the three-hour-plus production finished. I strolled the concourses of the Tate and the pavements of Fleet Street, peered through the locked gates of Lord's Cricket Ground in St John's Wood, and stood on a Westminster Bridge that Wordsworth would barely have recognised. On my own eccentric sightseeing tour I seemed never to cross paths with another sightseer.

This state of affairs was too much for the cabbie who drove me to Waterloo, where I was to take the Eurostar to Paris.

'Are long yew bin in Larnden, then?' he asked. Then, when I told him, he embarked on a long list of attractions.

His early questions were of the 'Wodger thinka Bucknam Palace?' kind, but as each in turn was parried with a helpless shrug he changed tack and adopted a 'Did yew go to … ?' approach. Puzzlement gave way to disbelief and exaggeration as we ticked off the must-see London sights I hadn't seen: Kew Gardens, Downing Street, St Paul's Cathedral, the Abbey. At last he exploded.

'Yew musta seen the Tar?' In the ensuing silence, the veins rose purple on his forehead and I feared he would have a stroke.

'Sorry,' I mumbled, staring out at the traffic. 'I haven't done very well, have I?'

That was my journey, but this is not. The itinerary (perhaps better called an agenda, in that word's literal Latin sense of 'things that must be done') is one compiled by the wonder and the wants of a lifetime much longer than mine. I need to help Mum find a London that may not exist – that may never have existed – outside the confines of her television screen. She wants to see a city that is the capital of a proud empire, a place where prime ministers are leaders and monarchs are honoured and neither is subject to comedians' ridicule and tabloid scrutiny. She wants to step back into a city where bombs whistle overhead and Churchill vows that 'We shall defend our island, whatever the cost may be … we shall never surrender.' We have four days to discover a London Mum will understand – and she can't walk.

Well, she can, after a fashion. The bionic hip is performing well, but the other one is showing signs of wear. I realise sickly that I have underestimated how much walking there is to do in the heat.

We pack as for a military expedition: in the kitchen of the small apartment I fill a thermos with tea and put slices of ham and cheese into small baguettes. A brick of Sainsbury's fruitcake gets wrapped in a paper towel. She puts up a bit of a fight when I tell her that her carefully chosen and packed shoulder bag will be staying in her room. I've already imagined an 80-year-old in a tug-of-war with a lean, strong street hood and decided that Mum is best burdened by nothing more than her walking stick and the nitrolingual spray for angina, which she thrusts down her bra.

It's not long before I wonder at the wisdom of this approach. Freeing her of responsibility for anything seems to make her irresponsible about everything. I quickly realise that all the walking she has done to get ready for this trip has been on the quiet, almost rural, roads near her home north of Auckland. There, outside rush hour at least, long minutes can elapse without a car passing; here the traffic is a constant gushing stream and she seems determined to deal with it by entirely ignoring it. With a shock I realise that I am in charge of a travelling companion with all the road sense of a slightly simple child.

She stumps along the pavement, each step punctuated with the belligerent rubber-metal thump-click of her collapsible walking stick. Staring fixedly at the ground before her – except when she ought to be, when the surface is broken and uneven – she marches unhesitatingly into flows of traffic from which I must grab her before she's bowled by a Royal Mail van or double-decker bus.

I should feel angry – and I do feel slightly exasperated. But I also feel sad. This was not the way it was meant to be. At the end of a long life of self-sacrifice, Mum deserves the dignity of being able to hop in a taxi without thinking twice about the cost. Instead she's still counting the pennies, scoffing at the suggestion that we might take a cab. It seems so unfair.

After much map-reading and decoding the system of bus stops, we point our bows at Cambridge Circus where we can get a bus to Whitehall and Westminster Pier. Charing Cross Road has none of the slightly musty charm it exuded the last time I was here. Where once browsers moved slowly between the shelves in bookshops, tilting their heads to read the writing on the spines, now most of the shops sell sex and cheap luggage and fake designer sweatshirts.

We thread our way through the roadworks – pneumatic drills chatter and flat-top trucks beep as they back up. Quickly I hit on a *modus operandi*: Mum walks ahead of me so I can see disaster approaching rather than have to turn round and deduce it *post facto*. This method of moving also slows me down – I am typically a brisk strider on city streets – and ensures that I match my pace to hers. Behind her, watchful, rather than ahead of her, chafing and impatient, I begin to see that walking slowly has its own pleasures. The displays in shop windows catch my eye and I have time to compose and then read the fanciful biographies of pedestrians walking towards me.

At last we reach the bus shelter. The seats are moulded plastic benches 20 centimetres wide, thigh-high and slightly sloping, the design brainchild of a clever transport planner who worked out how to make them impossible for the homeless to sleep on. Mum lowers her rump onto the orange plastic with a grunt and a sigh.

'We've come all the way from New Zealand,' she says. I snatch a look at her, wondering whether the heat, even this early in the morning, has hammered her into delirium, and realise with a start that she is addressing the couple alongside her.

They're West Indians and they turn their slightly bloodshot white eyes towards her and exhale in unison.

'Dart's a lawng wee,' says the man, making it sound as though New Zealand is a district of North London.

'Twenty-four hours,' Mum says proudly, and the West Indian couple hoot again and whistle with wonder.

'Dart's a laaaawwwng wee,' the man repeats, leaning on the adjective so that it becomes a slow, smoky exhalation of wonder. He hauls himself to his feet and scratches his white-singleted belly. A bus is approaching. It may be his. It may not be. He's taking it anyway, and his wife's in tow.

'Were they from Jamaica?' Mum says as we clamber on our bus a few minutes later.

'I've no idea,' I reply. 'I'd have to ask them.'

'Well, they looked like they were from Jamaica,' says Mum.

The man facing us a few seats away – he's so close I can smell his expensive eau de cologne and study the pink and cream skin beneath his impeccably manicured nails – is black, too. His belly does not stretch a white singlet though; he's wearing a suit, which impresses Mum hugely.

'It's marvellous, really …' she says (I'm not sure whether she's speaking to me or him and, what's worse, I doubt he is either, but there's no time to wonder as she ploughs headlong into the sentence) '… that the blacks have done so well. There aren't the racial problems here, you see.'

If the man in the suit has heard what Mum said, he gives no sign of it. Perhaps he is used to casual slights, even disguised as compliments.

We pour out onto the pavement at the foot of Whitehall, close to the seat of power, and head down Parliament Street past the Cenotaph. The sun seems to scorch my hairless head, and I mention to Mum that I need to keep an eye out for a hat.

As Big Ben comes into view, I pose like a conjuror who has just produced a rabbit from a scarf stuffed into a balled fist. It seems a defining moment, the first glimpse of the iconic St Stephen's Tower, a visible marking of the moment we have arrived. As it happens, it's only a few seconds until midday and we stand in what I hope might be wonder as the bell chimes (correctly, it is the bell, not the tower, that is named Big Ben).

'That wasn't twelve,' says Mum.

'You what?'

'I'm telling you that wasn't 12 chimes,' she repeats, waving her stick at the gilt face of the clock that traditionally sounds out GMT. 'I doubt it was more than ten.'

'We'd better alert them, then,' I say, taking her arm and leading her off in the direction of Westminster Bridge.

'I'm telling you,' she says, 'it wasn't twelve.'

Wordsworth's poem *Composed Upon Westminster Bridge, September 3, 1802* was something of a waypoint in my literary education. Its obscure sentimentalism appealed enormously, as did its mannered inversions ('Dull would he be of soul who could pass by / A sight so touching in its majesty'), which I deployed promiscuously in my own overblown teenage doggerel. But what I loved much more about the poem was the way it made a fool of our fourth-form biology teacher.

An irascible, red-headed Yorkshireman who stuffed his pipe stem-first down his walk socks, he was fonder than most of his colleagues (and all were quite remarkably fond) of humiliation as a control mechanism. That's why I so relish the memory of the day he was humiliated and quite unable to admit it. I'm not even sure that it was obvious to everyone; but it was obvious to me, and he knew it was, and that was all that counted.

He had arrived in class bearing under his arm one of those slender cases that contained a National Library Service 16-millimetre film. A murmur rippled across the laboratory, where we were all seated by sinks and gas taps for Bunsen burners and preparing ourselves for another session on the fundamentals of the circulatory system or the reproductive cycle of the earthworm. A film meant no work. We knew from early on it meant no work for the teacher, too, and that was mostly why he showed it. But we didn't mind. No work meant (probably) no homework. The day was looking up.

The film was called *All That Mighty Heart* and it was apparent after the first few frames that it was a film about the pulsing, pumping centre of the British Empire, London. The title was taken from Wordsworth's poem, describing the early morning peace, which ends with the words 'Dear God! The very houses seem asleep / And all that mighty heart is lying still.' The biology teacher, whose surname, Plant, was the cause of much amusement as we copied down notes on photosynthesis, had plainly grabbed the film from the shelf in the staffroom assuming that it would introduce his charges to the mysteries of human cardiology. As the tones of the narrator filled the laboratory, bouncing off beakers and retorts and brown carboys full of powders labelled with chemical names I would never understand, I turned slowly to look at the teacher, who was seated on a side bench at the back of the room. One foot was up on the bench, the knee under his chin. The other swung freely, just a little too fast, it seemed to me, to be casual. I maintained my gaze long enough to be sure that he knew I was looking, knowing. His gaze never shifted from the screen. It was a small moment of triumph in a long and bitter series of defeats.

As it happens, the two-hundredth anniversary of the writing of that poem is celebrated barely three weeks after I take Mum to stand on the bridge. Poets gather at the site, in the shadow of Big Ben, and the newspapers savour the irony of their reading a poem that mentions 'smokeless air' and 'a calm so deep' over the cacophony of traffic.

Their efforts are rewarded with wide coverage. Less noticed is a piece by an historian, pointing out that in 1802 high fences were erected along both sides of the bridge to discourage pedestrians from turfing rubbish (or perhaps themselves) into the tide. Wordsworth would have seen nothing from the bridge unless he'd been on the upper level of a horse-drawn carriage. The image of the poet, gazing in rapt tranquillity at the city 'all bright and glittering in the morning air', is another of the comforting fictions with which the English sustain their view of themselves.

Yet here we are, pushing our way through the summer crowds at Westminster Steps, past the souvenir hawkers and ticket touts, trying to get to a position in relation to the clock tower that will allow me to prove we made it. It feels faintly desperate, this sort of chore, and I'm not sure Mum appreciates the importance of the task since she is dawdling and peering at postcards.

'Hurry up,' I call, feeling both impatient with her and impatient with myself for being impatient.

She's not listening. She burrows into a knot of chattering

Asians and bum-bagged Americans and emerges like a miner from a pit, proudly wearing a floppy hat. It's little-boy blue and bears the legend 'London' and a picture of Westminster Palace.

'There y'are,' she says, with evident pride. 'How d'you like that?'

I realise she's thinking of my need for sun protection and I resist the urge to explain that melanoma will eat away my entire frontal lobe before I will wear a blue floppy with the Houses of Parliament on it.

'That's nice, dear,' I say, lobbing the hat back onto the stall's display table. 'Now stand over here while I take your photo.'

'Where are we going now?' she asks as we head back along Parliament Street.

'Shoosh! I'm looking at the map. Just keep walking.'

The Cabinet War Rooms on Horse Guards Road, the nerve centre of the campaign to defeat the Nazis, seems like the kind of place Mum would like to see. Here we can admire the chair on which Churchill sat as he directed proceedings in a group of rooms deep underground and reinforced against the German bombing. Fortunately, while it's underground, it's all on a single level so I wedge Mum into a wheelchair and we take up our audio guides.

This guide, an optional extra at most tourist sites, is a device which looks like a long television remote control and is designed to be held against the ear like a telephone. Fortunately these ones have a 'hands-free' kit, which allows me to clasp both handles of the wheelchair.

Dimly sensing the danger that lies ahead, but having no idea of its scope, I crouch down and speak to Mum as to a child.

'Now, Mum,' I say. 'When you press "99" and "play" it will give you ...'

'I know that,' she interrupts. 'He already told me that.' At this she begins peering long-sightedly at her guide and punching buttons at random.

'... instructions. Great. Now when you get to the end of those just pause for me and we'll try and set off at the same ...'

'Keep quiet!' she hisses. 'I'm trying to listen to the instructions!'

I sigh and do the same, wishing that I had a fast forward button so I could catch up.

'On the left … the first door,' Mum is saying. I drop into a crouch again.

'What I'm trying to explain, Mum …'

'Hurry up! We're missing it!' she howls. I snatch the guide from her and press the pause button.

'… is that if you pause, you should let me know you're paused and I'll pause.' (I realise that my voice is now a loud whisper dripping with frustrated rage and glance guiltily around.) 'That way we can keep roughly in sync with each other, and I won't have to kill you.'

One of the staff, seeing what he takes to be our helpless distress, approaches with what looks like it is going to be an offer of help. I swivel on him, flashing a baleful gaze of about zero Celsius, and he beats a retreat.

Mum notices none of this and can hear nothing I say because she isn't listening. I press the number for the first piece of commentary, thrust the guide back into her hand and give the wheelchair a vicious push that sends her lurching backwards. Undaunted she punches more buttons and claps the device to her ear.

'Heard that bit,' she says. For an instant I am gratified by the fact that she is speaking at a normal volume until I realise that she is talking to the man giving the commentary as though he is on the other end of a telephone. Then she turns to me and repeats 'HEARD THAT BIT!' at a volume that would alert listeners in Germany and I know everything is all right.

Thus our passage through the maze of rooms quickly becomes a silent battle of wills: Mum bellows out interesting tidbits of information, which I have digested seconds before or am just about to hear, as though she had made some profoundly significant original discovery. All the while I try to maintain a constant speed, remaining alert to Mum's body movements. If she swings around, gazing wistfully behind, I know she's just heard about something we've passed and I do a U-turn.

Alternatively, if she says something like 'What map table? I can't see any map table!', I am alerted to the need for acceleration. More commonly, though, she waves her stick above her head, like the commander of a cavalry regiment urging his horsemen into the charge and we move on.

The visitor to the War Rooms is constantly reminded that the place has been preserved precisely as it was, that everything except the fug of Churchill's cigar smoke is still there, though I've always felt such assurances are best regarded sceptically. Those who make their living in the past are often inclined to fudge the difference between preserving and recreating it. But what strikes me most is something easy to fake, but too trivial not to be true: three chipped and slightly grimy sugar cubes, which were found secreted in the back of an officer's drawer. It seems at once poignant and achingly banal that a man who worked on the top rung of the war machine should have been reduced to such subterfuge because of his want for simple luxuries. It seems so terribly English in a stiff-upper-lip, shoulders-to-the-wheel sort of way, especially since the very phrase 'war effort' rings so hollow in the twenty-first century. It's hard to imagine the generals at the Pentagon sipping on cheap bulk instant coffee so there would be more money for missiles to save the free world from Saddam Hussein.

We emerge, blinking like moles, into the bright sunlight. Mother is moved. Memories of the Blitz always had that effect. As a child I was always puzzled at the way Mum sat at virtual attention – she would have stood if it hadn't blocked the view of those behind – when old newsreels of London under attack flickered up on the cinema screen. It was history already, albeit recent, but my parents who were fond of living in the past because, as they liked to tell us, it was so much better than the present, seemed to look on it as current events. Mum gurgled with admiration for the defiant spirit of the bombed-out Brits. I lost count of how often she had reminded us that the King and Queen had stayed on in London as the bombs rained down and how pleased the Queen (who would become the Queen Mother) was when Buckingham Palace was bombed because, she said, 'Now I can look the East End in the eye.'

Whenever she told the story, it was in a tone of thinly veiled reproof, dripping with the implication that we didn't know how lucky we were. It always seemed to me slightly unfair to blame children for the fortunate circumstances of their childhood. We would not, presumably, have been to blame if our parents had raised us in a tea chest on waste ground alongside the railway lines. But the fact that we lived amid relative plenty on the edge of a prosperous provincial town in the 1950s in New Zealand seemed to make our every draught of breath an unimaginable impertinence. The King and Queen had dared death to rain down on them, our dad had endured five years of sand in his undies, our mother had pined for nylon stockings and sugar cubes and had spread dripping on her bread for four years, and we turned up our noses at Brussels sprouts.

'Oh, they were wonderful days,' says Mum, her eyes shining. 'They really were. I would have loved to live through the Blitz.'

We wander across Horse Guards Road and into St James' Park. The heat gathers and my backpack feels heavy. The park benches along the lake edge are full of young city workers sunning themselves. No one offers an old woman hobbling on a stick, or her even needier packhorse and travelling companion, a seat. Eventually we crush our way onto a five-person bench by shunting aside a couple of gossipy youngsters and I peel the paper towels off the baguettes.

Back at the flat, I lie down for a small nap and sleep more than three hours. I only wake when Mum, tiring of the waiting, comes out to the kitchen and starts putting away dishes with a calculated clinking. I groan and roll over.

'Time to get up,' she says, when I complain. 'You don't want to sleep the whole day away.'

The octogenarian is setting a pace her middle-aged son can't keep up with. Shaking my head clear, I pull my jacket on and we head out to eat.

FATE ACCOMPLI

Childhood lasted longer then, but for us it ended early. I can remember one of its last days. I am nine, and walking home from school for lunch. It's not far, a dozen houses or so, and more than 40 years later the taste of freedom is fresh on my tongue. I am wearing a velour sweatshirt the colour of tinned salmon, and its pile is soft to the touch and pleasant. The sun warms my back. I am barefoot. I feel the pebbles underfoot, the unevenness of an unpaved footpath whose edges are worried by weeds.

Mum has lunch ready, boiled eggs with fingers of cotton-wool-white bread from which the yolk droops and lands in orange-gold pools on the plate. Milk makes a moustache on my freckled upper lip. Outside, the back lawn, which seems to go on for ever, shimmers in the early summer heat. The chooks gurgle as they peck about in the cool shade of the orchard.

It feels like a holiday. When we settled in this part of town, the open road, whose beginning was marked by the white sign with the diagonal black slash, was only a few houses up the street. Now, as the growing city has crept out to meet us, a large subdivision of state housing has sprung up on a nearby pocket of open ground. The streets are all named after English poets – Dryden, Spenser, Coleridge and Shakespeare – although I will only notice this with years of hindsight and appreciate the irony that a subdivision that houses mainly Maori residents is threaded with streets named after very dead, very Pakeha writers.

The population explosion has meant a new school closer to home, and for the last term of my primary school life, I've been rezoned into it. My first few years have been in the hands of stern-faced men in short-sleeved shirts and narrow ties, their hair precisely parted and shining with Brylcreem. They keep thick leather straps, folded like giant tongues, in the top drawers of their desks. They use them, often, on children who hold trembling hands away from their bodies, flinching in advance and straining to calculate when to withdraw them from the descending leather. It is a fine art: go too early and the teacher will adjudge a blow too imperfect to count; go too late and the little hand will bear the full brunt. The perfectly timed flinch will let the hand ride the strap and the pain will scarcely register.

But here, at the new school, it is all different. Our teacher is a mousy and ineffectual Englishwoman with a squeaky voice who is probably only 45 but seems impossibly ancient. We sense her weakness and play up in ways we would have never considered at the last school. A normally well-behaved and studious youngster, I am easily swept up in the mood of miscreant mayhem that prevails. Perhaps, having seen my brothers going on before, I want to go wild while I still have the chance. I can see in them what is coming the next year, when colourful clothes and bare feet give way to caps and long socks and when the carefree will become suddenly careworn and seem to age overnight.

Certainly I enjoy the sense of seniority that comes with being in the final class. We are here only for a term, too short a time to settle in. It seems like a pause before the serious business of growing up.

The teacher, perhaps in an attempt to appease the boys, allows us to come to school heavily armed. We swagger through the school day with toy revolvers on our hips – although in an attempt to exercise some control the teacher quickly sets up a system whereby we lay our guns on the bench near the window where art materials are cut and mixed. We accept the restriction grudgingly, and only after we remind ourselves that real gunslingers sometimes had to check their weapons when they entered real saloons.

Classes are chaotic. The teacher struggles to make herself heard, much less obeyed. But when she pulls out her battered paperback copy of Ian Seraillier's *The Silver Sword* we settle down. We are all transported by the story of these three children in wartime Poland and because it is being read to us we don't realise that the name of the main character, pronounced 'Yarn', is spelt 'Jan'. We would have laughed if we'd read it because there is scarcely anything quite as funny as the idea that a boy might have a girl's name.

I have discovered the spelling of Jan's name because sometimes, being a good reader, I am allowed to read to the class. The teacher reasons that giving me that responsibility might tame my wildness and, indeed, the fact that I share this explosive secret with her gives me a brief flush of self-importance. I feel superior to my classmates because I know something they don't, something that would make them laugh if they knew and I will not give them the satisfaction of such juvenile amusement.

But if I am in a secret, grown-up club of two with the teacher, she doesn't seem to realise it. She cannot resist exacting a brief and humiliating revenge when she picks me up for pronouncing 'Polish' as 'polish'. 'Polish is what we put on the floor,' she sighs, looking round the room and encouraging laughter at my expense. 'It's Poe-lish.'

It's 1963. Almost a year has passed since the Cuban Missile Crisis, but the world of our imagination is ethnically divided along wartime lines into the Allies (including the benighted populations crushed under the Nazi jackboot) and the enemy. Britain is the centre; the cultural power of the late twentieth century's real imperial force has yet to be felt in these islands.

Our playtime, though, is full of American myths we learn in the dark at the movies, where our heroes wear buckskin and fight gibbering hordes of Plains Indians. At lunchtime we slip our guns into holsters and head for the badlands of the back fields. My holster – initially made for my elder brother, who has now had to put away childish things – is the work of a saddler patient of my father, a doctor whose grateful patients regularly do him favours. It's a beautiful object, handcrafted in thick leather. The back is rigid and the pocket supple and creamy white, but I feel faintly ashamed of it. I wish my parents would buy the *real* holsters I see on display in the toy shop.

Still, we are not quick-draw artists, so our pistols are always in our hands, spitting out dozens, even hundreds of shots without needing reloading. Anyone caught out and felled by the fifteenth and sixteenth consecutive rounds from a six-shot revolver will appeal in vain against the ballistic improbability of his fate. He must lie, face down and groaning, in the grass, the smell of freshly cut paspalum in his nostrils, and contemplate the attractive possibility that childhood will never end.

'Calder! Are you with us?'

The piece of chalk hits the side of my head, clipping the top of my ear. It smarts and, abruptly, the sun turns off. It's cold and damp in these classrooms where my predecessors' initials have been scratched into the stone walls with the points of geometry compasses. The desks are worn from use, stained with spilt ink, deeply carved with the names of former occupants. The cupped floorboards are thick with a patina of grime and wax and age. The smell is stale and greasy and sickly. It won't be long now before someone tells me that these are the best years of my life.

Southwell, one of the country's few preparatory schools, sits in forested grounds only a few hundred yards from my original primary school. The chalk thrower is a florid, rake-thin and sardonic psychopath called Cumming, the son-in-law of the headmaster whose father started the school as a private business a few years before the First World War. Mr Cumming wears circular horn-rims and a rumpled sports jacket covered in a fine dusting of chalk. He's really the school bursar, a glorified accountant, but he's regularly propped up in front of classes. It seems to have been taken for granted that there is a perennial shortage of teachers and that any warm body can take charge of a class whose parents are collectively paying several hundred dollars an hour in today's money for the privilege of sending their kids to a private school.

I am here because … well, I don't know why. My brothers were here before me and although they regularly came home with bloodcurdling tales of the brutality of school life, I was always going to come here, too. It's just assumed as the way it's going to be, a 'fate *accompli*' if you like, and a precursor to the real business of King's College, where my father and uncle and their father before them have gone.

My form teacher is a Mr Hulton, an immaculately turned-out Englishman in tooled brogues and tweed jacket whose mouth forms a thin, cruelly lipless line on his face. To us boys, baby-skinned and still piping in childish trebles, he seems like an unsmiling sadist. His hair is crew cut, making his head look rectangular from all angles. If he signed up with Central Casting he could easily play a Nazi, probably the one who struggles to restrain the slavering attack dog. Later, I will see him behind dark glasses at the wheel of his black FJ Holden, a classic car now, but one which must then have been near-new, and realise that he fancies himself as pretty cool. For now, though, he is the source of information – his speciality is biology – which he chalks on the board in sloping, regimentally even printing. We commit it like holy writ to the pages of our exercise books and then to memory.

Like most of the men placed in charge of firing my pre-adolescent imagination, he's probably a former officer in some branch of the British military. He may have studied at some university but what he's learned mostly is the importance of straight lines and following orders. And wherever they trained him he learnt the pedagogical power of a good thrashing. This he administers at the start of each day, in front of the class, *pour encourager les autres*. We return from learning the fear of God in morning chapel service to learn the fear of man, particularly when he is armed with a dense, metre-long, murderously flexible piece of cane.

This is a school where there are no detentions or lines; any infraction is punishable by a flogging. We often wonder what, if simply talking at the wrong time merits one savage stroke, a truly heinous offence might earn. In hushed tones we swap stories of a boy caught *in flagrante delicto* with a particularly lustrous young woman who worked in the dining hall. The event is probably a fiction conjured by imaginations through which testosterone is beginning to turn from pubescent trickle to adolescent gush, but it grows in the telling. I listen, awestruck as much by the young rooter's bravado as by the mysterious notion of carnal desire. In my mind, she cowers against the wall, clutching the crocheted bedspread modestly to her bosom. He glowers and growls at the authorities, who have come to take him away. He will – assuming he exists at all – be thrashed within an inch of his adventurous life and expelled. But, with his well-satisfied prick lolling against his prematurely hairy thigh, he knows he has already won.

The cane spends its days in a locker-size cabinet at the back of the classroom that also contains a skeleton. This grisly exhibit is meant to be a teaching aid, though no one can remember his ever having put in an appearance in front of the class, where he might have demonstrated the size of a femur or the complicated filigree of the metacarpals.

Instead, he stands guard over the instrument of torture, his eyeless face stripped of muscle and skin and frozen in a hideously toothy rictus. We almost swoon with horror at the popular wisdom that he was an Indian famine victim, though we never think to ask why an engraved plate on the cabinet door gives him the name of Obadiah, which can hardly be a common moniker on the subcontinent. Indeed, we would not have dared mention his name for fear of the instrument he guarded. By power of association he lends the instrument of punishment a deadly menace, which it exudes even from behind a closed door.

We sit in alphabetical order. My surname beginning with 'C', I sit against the eastern wall and will spend my schooldays staring down the neck of a boy called Bridge. My seat is only two desks in front of the skeleton in the closet. I can feel its chill, clammy breath on my back.

The man who wields the cane walks past me to fetch it, which he does most mornings, while the boys whose infractions have caught his eye over the past 24 hours wait near the door, shifting nervously from foot to sandal-shod foot as the blood drains from their faces. He passes me on his terrible mission, so close I can hear the soles of his brogues creak as they flex. The smell of his pungent aftershave billows over me and I cower, afraid of guilt by association.

It takes practice to learn how to deal with this morning ritual. For the first few weeks, we stare with a slack-jawed horror as youngsters, barely 10 years old, offer their buttocks to a man almost twice their size. The switch whistles and its arc ends in a smack, absorbed by cotton or, more protectively in winter, woollen short trousers and human tissue into a sound something like 'thhhat!'.

With time we learn to look away, to affect a minute interest in heading and dating the next fresh page of our exercise books.

But no familiarity will stop the reactive flinch, a little jump that, like any shock, is part pleasure, part horror.

I know what they are going through, since I have felt the cane's bite myself. The year before, a trembling first-year who still sings in an angelic boy soprano, I am sprung by this watchful avenger, who spots me speaking from the corner of my mouth as we stand in line to enter the chapel for the short daily service. The dreaded sentence 'See me after' is uttered, and I arrive outside his classroom to await my turn.

There the teachers gather daily, to exchange cigarettes and stories and watch Hulton's victims explode from the classroom door clutching their buttocks and struggling not to cry. When I arrive to submit meekly to execution, Hulton, presumably having a short list that morning, is in the group. He is smiling – something I have never seen him do – and the masters gathered round are smiling, too, as he shares a joke with them. He breaks off as he catches sight of me.

'Ah, yes, Calder,' he says.

I say nothing, not knowing what the correct response might be, although I briefly toy with the idea of falling to my knees, clutching his trouser cuffs and screaming for clemency. He hasn't finished his story. His audience is waiting expectantly. For an instant it seems I might be spared.

'See me after,' he says and turns away.

I walk disconsolately off, aware that the pain has been postponed but the sentence has not been commuted. But as I slink into class, I spot the frayed edge of a lifeline hanging from the end of his instruction. 'See me after,' he has said. After what? After class? After lunch? After Christmas, perhaps? After you have grown big enough to come back here with a baseball bat and pulverise my cuboid, lantern-jawed skull? The ambiguity is enough to give me an escape route. I will say nothing and, if called on, plead innocently that I didn't realise 'after' had arrived.

The days drag on and I manage to stay out of harm's – and Hulton's – way. Most of my days are spent in a distant classroom, far from his view. In chapel line, I am conscientiously though not ostentatiously silent. I stand in the inner queue, so that larger boys stand between me and the scanning eyes of the masters, and try to melt into the ivy that greenly cloaks the old brick wall. But the danger is not dead; it is only sleeping. Hulton runs my cricket team.

I am fielding just backward of square on the leg side, only a few yards from where Hulton stands as umpire. He is inscrutable behind the shades, but as the afternoon wears on I can feel myself loosening up. I begin to become convinced that he has permanently forgotten, or at least decided not to enforce, the punishment. Emboldened by this suspicion to the point of foolhardiness, I make a wisecrack about a teammate's play.

'Oh, do shut up, Calder!' Hulton says testily. I lapse into an anxious and, I hope, inconspicuous silence. But it is soon broken.

'Weren't you meant to be seeing me?' he asks, leaning on the 'seeing' to squeeze every last drop of baleful meaning from it.

'Yes, sir, only I …'

It is too late. He has extracted a small notebook from his pocket and is entering my name in his neat, italic printing.

'After chapel tomorrow,' he intones. I can feel the blood drain not just from my face but from my entire upper body. For a moment I feel like I'm going to evacuate my bowels – not a good idea when you are wearing baggy white shorts.

The next morning as I arrive at his room, Hulton sees me coming and peels off the group of smokers and laughers. I follow him up the three steps into the classroom. He strides, soles creaking, towards Obadiah's lair. None of the boys gives me so much as a glance; all are heading and dating the page of an exercise book. Perhaps some of them will have written the date twice, or wrongly, but when that's noticed, no one will connect it with the distraction that was occurring as they performed the task.

No doubt somebody has attempted to decode the psychosexual subtext of a form of punishment that requires a pre-pubescent boy to offer his buttocks to a grown man so that they may be beaten. It would be a brave teacher in these hysterical days, when any form of touch has been ruled inappropriate in the pedagogical relationship, who would admit that this obscenely ritualised form of punishment inspired in him the stirrings of sexual arousal, but the very idea lends a pungent double entendre to the hoary old line that 'This is going to hurt me more than it will hurt you.' In any case, anyone who ever said that line is either a liar or was never caned.

Years later in the film version of Henri Charrière's *Papillon*, I would see on the screen an image of my face as it must have appeared at the moment I bent before a man who was meant to be educating me. The unforgettable shot is taken from below, at the level of the basket that would catch the severed head, of a man being thrust into the guillotine and the wooden yoke being dropped, holding him in place. He gibbers and dribbles. Worse, in his eye is a kind of sickening resignation, which seems to strip him of all humanity. The last shabby dignity of fighting for his life is gone, and it's plain that it's gone because he is face down, presenting his buttocks to his tormentor, signalling submission in exactly the way our simian forebears did.

None of this, of course, goes through my mind as I bend over. I am fighting the urge to faint. I hear the cane before I feel it. It swishes and whistles and thwacks. A long instant passes. Then my arse is on fire. I rocket from the room howling – I use the word here not as a synonym for crying but literally to convey the noise that dogs make at the full moon – and as I pass by the knot of masters, they erupt into gales of laughter. It may be coincidence – perhaps someone has cracked a good joke at the moment that I sweep past – or they may have been laughing at my distress. Either way, it seems pretty sick.

Across the quadrangle, at what seems an impossible distance, my best mate Paul Gilmour waits. He is risking punishment himself by staying out of class to comfort me. Even at that distance I can see the expression on his face, the lips pursed into a silent whistle, solicitous and empathetic. He hustles me into an empty classroom and nurses me through the first, terrible minute or two as the pain peaks and begins to subside. The tears – a sign of unmanliness that would be scorned at any other moment – flow freely and Paul makes no effort to stop me crying. Eventually I pull myself together sufficiently to hobble off to class, Paul walking alongside me, nursing me along as he would a war-wounded.

A boy who still takes a cloth-eared rabbit to bed has his buttocks crossed by a purple and yellow welt for 10 days. If any parent had thought to ask why they were paying good money to have their children endure – or, at the very least, watch – such brutal assaults, the teachers would have said that a regular public caning had a powerful deterrent effect. It improved morale and, consequently, performance. It's hard to argue with that. If they'd shot a couple of juniors each day and disembowelled their limp corpses on a gibbet in the quadrangle, the school could have pumped out more Nobel laureates.

Looking back it is impossible to believe we were in New Zealand. The school was called Southwell; the 'w' was silent and it rhymed with 'trouble', and we soon learned to deride as incurably provincial anyone who pronounced it wrongly. It was a perfect facsimile of an English prep school. We wore our striped blazers and caps, called our masters 'sir' and thought nothing of the fact that they called us only by our surnames. Sometimes a new boy (the two words were amalgamated in common parlance into one, 'newboy', which was pronounced as one might utter the name of a fungal infection) would betray his novice status by addressing a long-standing friend by his given name. A sudden silence would descend, heads would swivel, all eyes would bore in on the perpetrator of this solecism. It was a moment I would recognise when I came across Bateman's cartoons, like 'The man who asked for a scotch and soda in the Pump Room at Bath'. Maybe the silence would be broken by a voice saying 'We don't use Christian names here,' but usually it was not necessary. The authority of the pack had been reasserted, the distasteful idea of individuality erased. Surnames it was.

If there were two of us by the same name we were numbered, in Roman numerals, of course; pity Smith VI. But even that was an act of colonial modernism: we heard tell of schools in England where junior and senior siblings were called 'Major' and 'Minor' and we racked the parts of our little brains where our fledgling knowledge of Latin was stored to wonder, even with the superlatives of 'maximus' and 'minimus' to call on, how that system would accommodate six of the same name.

Annually we shouldered and carried the school tradition of

staging comic operettas by Gilbert and Sullivan, two stuffy Victorian Londoners who mixed music hall and opera into a very English confection all their own. The fascination with these works was not the preserve of private schools, of course; no repertory company at the time would think of assembling an annual playbill that didn't contain one of the G & S classics. But for schools, and particularly private schools, G & S was mandatory, and well into the 1970s I would find it odd that a school might produce Thornton Wilder's *Our Town* or the work of some unknown by the name of Bruce Mason instead of making what seemed like the natural choice.

I played the goonish jailer Wilfred Shadbolt in the 1965 production of *The Yeomen of the Guard*. My eldest brother, playing the lugubrious Tower of London watchwoman, Dame Carruthers, in the 1958 version, had sung lines which contained concentrated spoonfuls of a history I swallowed as my own, and I heard them again with relish:

When our gallant Norman foes
Made our merry land their own
And the Saxon from the Conqueror were flying.

Not until several years later would I have any idea who Normans were, never mind these chaps called the Saxon and the Conqueror. But at a level I could never have expressed at the time, I was cementing in the notion of who I was: a little Englishman, learning to do my bit to make a little bit of England in this green and pleasant land.

Out on the eastern field, we are playing cricket. Our coach is an Englishman who rejoices in the name of Major Gay, but these are innocent times and ours are innocent minds: his surname inspires none of the smutty double entendre it now would. In any event, he is the very model of the boisterously British and unquestionably heterosexual manhood for which we are being prepared: a military man who, it is rumoured, was once twelfth man for the MCC.

At the Masters vs First XI match, he strikes an impressive

figure in his cream flannels and scrupulously whitened leather cricket boots, which rasp metallically on the concrete in the pavilion. We boys wear baggy creased cotton shorts stained with the old marks of desperate dives in the outfield.

The Major is a figure no satirist could invent. The eyes, set deep in a face lined with burst capillaries, seem constantly to be scanning the horizon for German tanks or perhaps bands of marauding Zulu. He smokes a pipe, which juts permanently from his mouth, except when he grasps it in a liver-spotted hand with fingertips tanned to the hardness of saddle-leather by repeatedly tamping white-hot wads of tobacco. The other hand, white-knuckled, is closed around a spring-loaded device which, when kept permanently compressed, is designed to toughen the wrists to titanic strength.

The Major never misses an opportunity to underline the importance of the wrist. He's fond of recalling an innings the year before by the tubby English batsman Colin Cowdrey. In a test match at Lord's, Cowdrey's arm was broken by the West Indian speedster Wes Hall, but he returned to the crease and helped save the match with a one-armed and unbeaten nineteen.

'Like this, d'you see?' the Major would say and, grabbing a size five bat from one of his tiny listeners, would mime a slow-motion, one-armed leg glance or late cut and then hold the bat aloft to salute an invisible crowd as he reached his half century.

I am padded up and waiting my turn at bat, standing near the boundary with Major Gay and my father. They are swapping war stories. Anxious and fretful, I decide to readjust the straps on my pads. I hold out my gloves and bat to the Major.

'Would you hold these, please, sir?'

His pose, one hand on hip, the other around his pipe bowl, doesn't change. 'No, I will *not* hold them,' he replies without missing a beat. 'Put them on the ground.'

As I stoop to obey him I hear my father laugh, an appreciative cackle of ascending cadence which he has always reserved for jokes in which someone has humiliated another by being smarter or more knowledgeable. It's an expression of solidarity with his fellow adult, his fellow army veteran, his fellow Englishman. He is expressing his approval at the act of casual dismissiveness he calls discipline, his admiration for the way the Major has so elegantly guided my full-pitched but wayward impertinence to the boundary. He is enjoying the fact that the Major is giving me what my parents have paid for: he's teaching me that kids should know their place. I flush with shame and a sense of betrayal. But what hurts most is my failure to realise that for my father – who never comes close to saying, 'Here, son, give them to me' – family loyalty comes a distant second to proper form.

Harold Reginald Hornsby, MA (Oxon), is a Gurkha first and a classics scholar second. He is known, with no great affection and certainly not to his face, as 'Jerk' for his rather violent limp, which, it is darkly rumoured, is the result of a war wound. At times I am sure he would rather be teaching us how to go hand to hand with a gibbering Jap, stripped to the waist in the steaming jungle. Instead, it is his calling to make something of us by leading us, stuttering and stumbling, through Caesar or Virgil. Here we get to see the arcane constructions we have learned from textbooks pressed into service to describe complicated military manoeuvres. Called on by name to translate at sight, we trace along the lines of text that might as well be hieroglyphics as we assemble sentences word by word without any idea what any of them mean.

'... in order that the second legion might attain the summit?' trills a boy soprano, the rising inflection betraying his uncertainty.

'Well, for goodness' *sake*, boy!' Hornsby explodes, tearing his glasses from his face and sending them skittering across the desk. They come to rest against a box of Stephens' chalk and, after a long second's pause, the momentum dies away and a lens falls out with a clearly audible plink. No one laughs.

'For goodness' *sake*,' he is saying. 'What *else* can he do?' He swivels on his good leg and, his black cape swirling, lurches towards the blackboard.

'Here the enemy hordes are arrayed!' The chalk makes a scything arc and breaks so that his small, girlish fingernails rake with a hideous squeak across the dusty surface.

We wince or shriek, but he warms to his subject. 'The first legion, tired after a long march and hugely outnumbered, does not want to launch an attack into the setting sun.' Rays of light, more squeaking fingernails. 'What hope can the generals have except to outflank, outflank, outflank, OUTFLANK?' With each repetition, the chalk squeaks again, driving arrows into the heart of the heathens from a hilltop which we, quite lost in the trackless expanses of subjunctives and ablatives, had never noticed.

He picks up the spectacles and hurls them at his face where they lodge only slightly skewed, one arm high on the close-shaven side of his head. He peers half over, half through them, apparently unaware that a lens is missing and glares around the class to pick the next translator.

Hornsby had come to St Paul's from Christ's College, whose pupils, twerpish in ties and boaters, seemed risibly English even to us. He, it was adjudged, was the man for the job of making the country's newest private school its best. In doing so, he gathered around him a staff of men more than half of whom were expatriate Englishmen. Some had arrived via colonies in Africa, which they referred to unblinkingly as 'the Dark Continent', allowing the inference that they were lucky to have escaped it. Others were, presumably, escapees from the bleak privations of post-war England who must have wondered what strange land they had fetched up in, among these strapping milk-fed lads in the wide-open Waikato.

The First XV was coached by an ex-Royal Navy man, a mathematician. He insisted that the entire school turn out to support the mud-stained warriors at home games and decreed that barracking was to take the form of 'Come on, School' or simply, cryptically, 'School', which was presumably to be accompanied by an exclamation mark. Some of us wondered privately whether the opposition, which was always a school, might not be heartened by the mistaken assumption that they were the object of this arcane encouragement. But it didn't do to question this man's word. He had a foul temper, which would, without warning, send him into a beetroot-red and spittle-flecked rage.

He was midget-sized, smaller than all but the tiniest first-years, a fact that doubtless prompted his standing rule – well, really a sitting rule: we were to ignore the normal procedure by which the class would rise when its master entered; nor was a seated boy to rise and approach him for assistance, but rather to raise his hand and wait to be approached.

The most English of the lot was one James Danvers Baker, a born-and-bred Kiwi who, we were told, had returned from a fortnight's holiday in Britain speaking like Laurence Olivier in *Brideshead Revisited*. He dressed like a squire on a grouse shoot – shooting stick, deerstalker hat and rubber galoshes – and referred to his subject, geography, as 'joggers'. Whether he enjoyed teaching or not, none of us knew, since he did so little of it. But he plainly loved smoking, since he spent whole classes doing that. As his blue exhalations filled the shafts of winter sunlight angling in through the high classroom windows, he would sneeringly tell us that Harewood was actually pronounced Harwood and said 'pounds' (these were pre-decimal days) the way Prince Charles did, so that it rhymed with 'finds'.

Although we were aware that our education was in the hands of distinctly weird individuals (with the passage of time I have come to see some of them as profoundly disturbed, at least emotionally and in some cases psychiatrically), our parents seemed happy to pay the equivalent of tens of thousands of twenty-first-century dollars for the privilege. But in the midst of it all, this Englishness fascinated and entranced me and even as my cynicism about school grew with seniority, I never questioned the assumptions about the endlessness of Empire that underlaid it.

I was instantly smitten when a young Englishman arrived as a house tutor. The very system of house tutoring was an index of our adherence to Mother England: it provided free bed and board for an English school leaver in what was, and still is, known as his 'gap' year in return for light babysitting duties so the salaried masters could have the night off. Prince Edward was one of the system's alumni, slumming it at Wanganui Collegiate for a year in the 1970s.

The youngster – for that was what he was, only a year or

two older than me – was an old boy of Fettes, a private school in Edinburgh, whose alumni – perhaps, now I think about it, a contemporary of his – included British Prime Minister Tony Blair. A grey-eyed slightly goonish figure with shoulders permanently bent in a resigned stoop, he peered out from a face spectacularly festooned with acne pustules and proclaimed his seniority by smoking heavily whenever we were around.

I spent hours in this man's cramped bedsit in one of the boarding houses, partly because it had been deemed I would learn the fundamentals of ancient Greek from him. We sat in deco armchairs working our way through the alphabet and the present tense of the verb 'to be'. I gave up Greek shortly afterwards – it was never so much an academic interest as part of an image of myself as an Oxbridge undergraduate in the making – though I can still recite and even write that alphabet. But I was learning something else in that smoke-fugged room over cups of sweet instant coffee. The English house tutor interspersed moments of legitimate tuition with stories of Fettes and filled my head with stories of life in a real 'public' school. I was entranced with the idea of leaving these mediocre and provincial shores and making my way in my spiritual home.

NOT REALLY LOST

If this is Tuesday, this must be St Paul's Cathedral. The dome that dominated the riverfront in the Thames Television logo is now hemmed in by high-rise office blocks, but most antipodeans still make the trek to the top of Ludgate Hill to see where the Prince of Wales married a blushing pre-school teacher from Kensington.

But that memory holds no great charm for Mum, who regards the dead princess less than charitably ('a little minx' is the conclusive opinion, I seem to remember). She feels a link with the cathedral because its long-time Dean, Martin Sullivan, was a local lad, a man intimately bound up with the Auckland Anglican church.

Getting to St Paul's means a change of buses at Trafalgar Square, which Mum had expressed interest in. 'I want to go to Trafalgar Square so I can see a bag lady,' she had said, though under cross-examination it emerged that it was a 'bird lady' like the one in *Mary Poppins* she was wanting to see. (I briefly explained what a bag lady was and she looked at me as though I was pulling her leg before whistling and whispering 'Poor devils'.) What's more, I said, Mary Poppins' bird lady was at St Paul's – I proved my point by crooning the first four bars of the song – and I imagine she would have been moved on by now, since Mary Poppins cast her spells over London in the days when suffragettes were chaining themselves to railings.

If the bird lady tried to feed the pigeons in Trafalgar Square these days, Mr Plod would run her in. The status of these birds seems to have plummeted since I was last here. Then, hawkers sold breadcrumbs (for a good deal more than tuppence a bag) so tourists could wade through waves of cooing, pecking pigeons; now, signs warn us not to feed the birds. I've bought the remains of some breakfast toast and the stub-end of the slightly stale loaf from which it was sliced. Sitting on the benches on the northern side, I steal a glance to see whether any uniforms are in sight and begin sprinkling the bits of bread.

'Ooooh,' hoots Mum, in a parody of the 'I'm going to tell the teacher' sound kids make. 'You're going to get in trouble.'

Beside me a young backpacker with a koala on her T-shirt smiles encouragingly. The pigeons are around me now, a thick carpet of pecking, some standing on my toes to be closer to the source of supply.

'Here, give me a bit,' says Mum.

'You'll get in trouble,' I reply, tearing off a crust.

Afterwards we wander around the square, gazing at statues of old dead guys whose military successes in the Levant or on the Indian subcontinent assured them of their place in history, or at least in the square. I accost a mother-and-daughter couple and ask if they'll take a photo of us.

'No worries,' replies the younger woman.

'Are you Australian?' I ask.

'No, Kiwis,' she says. I am about to chide her for using such a conspicuous Australianism, but I realise that phrase has crossed the Tasman now. It's just that suddenly, irrationally, it seems important to me that we – I mean she and I – celebrate our distinctiveness from Australia (even 'No probs' would have been better) as well as from this land, which was the home of our forebears but is not ours. The double-decker buses growl away from the kerb in front of the National Gallery. The lions stand guard around the column that supports the statue of a man as remote from my experience as Aristotle or Genghis Khan. What, I ask myself, am I doing here?

Trafalgar Square is being remade to take traffic away from one of London's most popular tourist stops. It will eventually make it quieter, and restore some sense of atmosphere to a place that has become one of the city's noisiest traffic islands. For now, though, it's an auditory nightmare, and it takes us a while to negotiate the street crossing and head for the bus.

Entering the Strand, I begin the process, now gradually becoming familiar, of working out which of the bus stops serves the line we want. I walk ahead of Mum, fretting at how far we have to go. She plugs along – taking the occasional breather on street-level window ledges or in bus shelters, reaching for the angina spray often enough to make me anxious. The bus takes us along into Fleet Street, which was where all the British national dailies had their headquarters until a larrikin Australian by the name of Rupert Murdoch took on the print unions. Now the papers are scattered all over inner London. The *Guardian* and its Sunday sister the *Observer* aren't far away, in Farringdon Road. But Murdoch's titles – the *Sun*, the *News of the World*, the *Times* and the *Sunday Times* – are in Wapping, at the western end of the Docklands just east of Tower Bridge; Express Newspapers is on the south side of the river at Blackfriars; and the Mirror Group is further east again at Canary Wharf. Only the international news and picture agency Reuters maintains a presence in the heart of what used to be newspaper land.

The bus rumbles up Ludgate Hill – barely perceptible as an incline these days, although it must have looked more clearly like a slope when it was named and nothing on it was more than a couple of cramped and grimy stories high. We can glimpse the familiar dome only through a canyon of tower blocks. And as we pile off the bus I see that, hard up against St Paul's, almost at the north-western corner of the great steps, the lower floors of an office and apartment building rise from a muddy, noisy building site. It's called, with no great originality, St Paul's, and Mum is charmed to see that the hoarding that hypes the project includes the words 'If you require a monument, look around you.'

'That's what's written on John Logan Campbell's grave on One Tree Hill,' she says. 'They've got a cheek pinching it.'

I start to chuckle and suddenly realise she is serious. The reference, hijacked by an advertising copywriter, is to the epitaph for the architect of St Paul's, Sir Christopher Wren. It was penned – by his son – in Latin, of course, but no PR firm would write *si monumentum requiris, circumspice* on a modern advertising hoarding for fear of being thought elitist.

I have seen Logan Campbell's grave often enough to know that its version of the epitaph is in the original Latin. But I know what it means because I stared at the words at my school when I was only eleven. They were on a bronze plaque in the small cramped chapel. There, where little New Zealand boys were made into ersatz Englishmen, the plaque remembered the school's founder. It isn't until I stand at the foot of the steps at the front of St Paul's that I realise just what a pompous and self-aggrandising gesture that was.

Mum sits on the stairs and I pour us a couple of cups of tea from the thermos. There is no sign of a bird lady in op-shop clothes and a tea-cosy bonnet. The stairs swarm with Asian and American tourists carrying expensive videos and pencil-thin Italian women in designer sunglasses, talking on tiny mobile phones and trailing slipstreams of expensive perfume.

We finish our tea and Mum rolls onto her hands and pushes herself slowly and painfully to her feet. It irritates me that she is still refusing my help – I repeatedly hold out my hand to her and offer to pull her upright but, determined not to be a burden, she keeps refusing.

We wander in the high door and Mum stops at the barred gates of a small memorial. A marble figure lies prone on a raised plinth, but there is no inscription to indicate who it is.

'Looks like Kitchener to me,' she says.

'Don't be silly,' I hiss through clenched teeth. 'Of course it's not Kitchener.'

We move further in, where guides in solemn ecclesiastical garb wander slowly with their hands behind their backs. One passes nearby and I attract his attention.

'We were wondering who the memorial is to, there on the left as you come in.'

'A very good question, suh, if I may say so,' he replies, stalling for time. 'That there is … it's, um …'

'Oh, I don't know,' grumbles Mum, turning away and shaking her head. 'Looks like Kitchener to me.'

The guide's eyes light up.

'That's it, ma'am,' he says, with a smile. 'Kitchener, that's 'im.'

I manage to mumble something approaching an apology, but the damage is done and I feel angry and ashamed at myself. I wonder when, and why, I stopped believing in my mother as a person who knew anything useful – or anything at all. As a little boy I relied on and never doubted her competence. She could make things work which were broken or bent. She could rout marauding neighbourhood bullies. And she knew the answers to things – maybe not the big questions, but when you're little it's the little questions that are big.

At some point, when I'd assimilated enough of the education for which she had sacrificed so much, I left her behind and I did so with more scorn than gratitude. Now, here in London, I'm wanting to share with her the largeness of a world she has only seen on the telly. I get impatient with her determination to reduce everything to fit into the dimensions of her own experience. I tell myself that in her resolve to be unimpressed, she has no sense of wonder. But perhaps her wonder is greater than mine. Self-consciously knowing, endlessly worldly, perhaps I am the one who is determined to be unimpressed, or at least to demonstrate how much bigger I am than my own sense of wonder; she, meanwhile, is showing the real human reaction to wonder, which is to make it manageable.

As if to ram the point home, as we move further into the airy interior I immediately find myself unimpressed. I am uncomfortably aware of the number of cathedrals I have been through and how – largely because of my ignorance of church architecture and ecclesiastical history – my eyes glaze over.

On the south side, near a door that gives a clear view of the new Millennium Bridge, are the steps that lead to the Whispering Gallery. The man guarding the door regrets that Mum cannot – and therefore may not – ascend, so I leave her prowling the nave and bound up the stairs – more than 250 of them. Halfway up, my legs ache and my lungs heave, but I refuse to slow. Like a small boy, anxious to impress his mother below with how big and strong he is, I power on. I burst out into the gallery where the geometry reportedly allows a whisper on one side of the huge dome to be heard by someone on the other side who puts an ear near to the wall. But there's no one to whisper to me. Mum is a speck in the front row of the nave far below, lounging slightly to one side to take pressure off her hip and gazing around her. For a moment I am seized by the desire to do a 'Look at me, Mummy!' wave but I feel faintly silly.

She looks so alone and bereft there and I wonder what's

going through her mind; perhaps she is lost in the regret that she is making this trip with her son. She might have rather travelled with the husband whose financial security she had contributed so much to.

'Are you back already?' she says, gathering her stick and groaning to her feet. 'That was quick. I looked for you and couldn't see you. Why didn't you wave?'

We eat lunch in a small park opposite the cathedral. There is only a single space on a park bench and I crouch on the concrete path, dealing Mum out bits of food. Again I'm struck by how the roles of parent and child are reversed. I am careful to ensure that she gets the better bit of cake, the second cup of tea, the tidier, less crushed baguette. She coos to the elderly women next to her how good I am being to her, how I won't let her carry anything, how tired I must be.

After lunch we head for Covent Garden. I know she's expecting to see Eliza Doolittle in grubby voluminous skirts and tattered bonnet, hawking flowers and dropping aitches and I haven't the heart to tell her that it won't be like that. But the sight of her face when we reach the market makes me wonder about whether I should have prepared her better.

'It's all new!' she says in evident disappointment, pronouncing the word like it's the name of a communicable disease.

In fact, 'new' may not be the word for it. The market is pure eighties kitsch, a tourist trap full of fussily detailed stalls and shops selling souvenirs and overpriced second-rate clothing.

We pause briefly to watch an acrobatic busker in the courtyard but there's nowhere to sit. Mum's anxious that we are not late for the matinee of *The Mousetrap*, which starts at 2.45 p.m. in the nearby St Martin's Theatre.

'Relax,' I tell her, brandishing the map book. 'I know exactly where we are. It's just through there.' I wave a hand airily in the direction of Shaftesbury Avenue.

We wander around for a while and glimpse the façade of the Theatre Royal, Drury Lane, where *My Fair Lady* is playing. The fact that Alfred Doolittle is being played by Dennis Waterman from *Minder*, who has always been a youngster in Mum's mind, seems faintly sacrilegious. I share with Mum a sense of proprietary jealousy about the show that was so much part of my growing up. The 33 rpm recording with Julie Andrews and Rex Harrison, its cardboard sleeve almost sliced into two sheets by repeated use, was part of the standard repertoire on the family's record player, and I knew most of the songs by heart long before I knew what many of the words meant. Certainly I had no understanding of what was implicit in the final exchange ('Oi washed my fice 'n' 'ands before Oi came, Oi did'; 'Eliza … where the devil are my slippers?'). Sex and love were mysteries, and the problem of sex roles hadn't been invented; I certainly would not have dreamt of questioning why a woman ought to know where a man's slippers are.

For a brief stabbing moment, as so often on this trip, I feel keenly the sense of how time – or change, which is just another name for the same thing – corrodes our sense of the way things ought to be. Childishly, petulantly, I want *My Fair Lady* to have Rex Harrison and Julie Andrews in it. I don't want to be almost as old as the man playing Alfred Doolittle in the West End.

We wander out into the street and peer through the doors of the Royal Opera House before strolling back through the market and heading down the nest of streets that lead towards St Martin's Theatre.

It should have been simple. The theatre is on West Street, one of several that radiate out from Cambridge Circus where Charing Cross Road meets Shaftesbury Avenue. I've approached it often enough from the other direction – Cambridge Circus is only a couple of hundred metres south of the Tottenham Court Road tube station and is where we take the bus each morning, where Mum ambushed the wide-eyed West Indians. So we are moving only slowly through the oppressive heat when, to my considerable consternation, I suddenly find we're out on a busy main road again.

Slightly disoriented, instead of looking at the map book I decide to ask someone for directions. But in a momentary lapse of judgement I ask for 'the way to Leicester Square'. Seven minutes of slightly anxious ambling later, I find I'm where I asked to go, in the crowded expanse of the huge, busy square I shouldn't even have been looking for.

Slightly panicked now – it's gone 2.30 p.m. – I head north, verbally dragging Mum behind me. Her progress is agonisingly slow, and I can see she's biting her lip as the pain flares in her hip. I'm cursing myself at an error that would have been a mild inconvenience if I'd been travelling alone (you're in a hurry, you run) but has turned into the makings of a full-scale nightmare now. I feel like I've let her down. Feeling so cocksure of my whereabouts and how to get to the theatre, I have left us too little time.

Half-heartedly, keenly aware of the futility of the gesture, I wave down a taxi, which is crawling along a clogged street that runs one way, the opposite direction from where we are headed.

'St Martin's Theatre,' I bark. 'Can you get us there in five … well, actually, four minutes?'

I'm half hoping that I'm more lost than I realise, that he'll tell us we're standing in front of it, but he dashes my hopes by looking over his shoulder and up the clogged street. The afternoon heat leans on me.

'I dunno, guv. Time I get rahnd the block and back up there, you'd be quicker to walk.'

'I've got her, though,' I say, jerking my head in the direction of Mum, who is still pounding the pavement towards us.

'She's all right,' he says, admiringly. 'Look at 'er go.'

In another situation, I might have found his expression of admiration sweet, even comical. But I'm about to explode. The cabbie sees this and his smile disappears.

'Look,' he says. 'Left here at the end of the street and straight up. But not as far as the circus. Litchfield you're looking for, on your right. Then you're there.'

'Can we make it by quarter to?' I beg.

'Not if you stand rahnd 'ere gassing to me,' he says. 'Gorn. Git going. Mum's leavin' you be'ind. Remember: Litchfield.'

I feel like kissing him and kissing whoever came up with 'The Knowledge'. Black cab drivers have to have detailed knowledge of 25,000 streets within a 6-mile radius of Charing

Cross: where we are going is barely 100 metres from The Knowledge's ground zero.

I battle through the crowds on Charing Cross Road, sneaking a glance behind from time to time to check that Mum is still with me. She is plodding now and panting, but maintaining her painful pace.

At 2.41 p.m. we are standing opposite Litchfield and I fairly drag Mum across the street, daring the cars not to stop. As we enter the street I let go her hand and run on ahead to pick up the tickets.

We make our seats with seconds to spare. What's more, the stalls are quarter-full and there's no obvious sign that the theatre pursues a policy of excluding latecomers.

But the incident has shaken me up, more than it has upset her. Charged with the task of getting her to the theatre on time, of keeping our sole appointment in a visit almost free of deadlines, I have put her through the one thing she is ill-equipped to handle: walking at speed along crowded streets. Not for the first time, I remind myself that I'm the responsible adult now, and that someone else is relying on me.

The Mousetrap is corny, camp and fun. The theatre is barely one-third full, but the actors do their best to breathe life into an old-fashioned whodunit. The story, like the set decor, is pure Christie: Detective Sergeant Trotter arrives at snowbound Monkswell Manor in Berkshire with grim news. A murder has occurred in London and he has reason to suspect another is imminent – in the manor, which is crowded with sudden arrivals. Depending on the angle of view, each of the seven guests seems suspect.

This is theatre from the age of the footlight. The lines are declaimed by a cast that is often arranged laterally, like birds on roosts, across the stage. Actors virtually wink if called on to deliver a line with a clue embedded in it. And the audience plays along: we brace ourselves for the gunshot – yet when it arrives we giggle rather than flinch.

The denouement involves a hat box from Harrods, but the resonances set up by the name of the Knightsbridge store owned by Mohammed Al Fayed make the reference odd and awkward. By the time the cast joins hands for a rather offhand bow and we are enjoined as 'members of *The Mousetrap* family' to keep its secrets, it feels faintly like being caught in a time warp.

Outside afterwards, we dawdle as I try to compose a photo of Mum in front of the theatre. As we finally move away up the street we bump into Peter Yapp, who plays the extravagantly suspicious Mr Paravicini.

'Good show, mate,' I say. For an instant I want to correct myself. 'Good show', after all, means something very different in an antipodean accent than in an upper-class English one.

He smiles his thanks and stops to chat. Tugging on a cigarette, the edge of his roughly removed make-up plainly visible at his hairline, he thanks us – a shade effusively I think – for coming. Twice during the subsequent conversation, he uses the phrase 'if we make it' to refer to the show's upcoming golden jubilee.

The doubt seems misplaced. *The Mousetrap*, which marked its fiftieth anniversary on November 25, 2002, would have reached that mark if it had been playing only to the ushers. Long ago, it became nothing more than the sum of its numbers. It became the longest-running production in British history on April 12, 1958 when it passed the five-and-a-half-year record of *Chu Chin Chow*, and the longest running in the world more than a quarter-century ago in the mid-seventies. The promoters say 'more than 10 million' have seen it; although that figure may be overstated, since it implies about 95 per cent houses and long flat box-office periods have often been remarked on.

In any case, only those who have never been to any other play would be likely to regard it as a good, or even interesting, piece of theatre. It long ago became much more – and much less – than that: a record-breaking curiosity, a fixture on the tourist circuit and a legendary part of theatrical folklore.

Even before you enter St Martin's Theatre, everything about *The Mousetrap* proclaims its determination to be assessed not for what it is but for how long it has been it. The pink neon sign, half the size of the theatre frontage, has the name of the author

– one Agatha Christie – in smaller letters than the words recording the length of the show's run. In the small foyer the crimson carpet is threadbare in places and a scoreboard-style counter (which on the night of the fiftieth anniversary read 20,807) marks the number of performances. 'This isn't the theatre, dammit!' everything seems to say. 'Why, it ain't even show business. This is History.'

In this pageant the front-of-house staff play their parts with a faintly distracted air, like old troupers working from an ancient script; a small souvenir stand sells sweatshirts and mugs and – oddest of all – *Mousetrap* mousepads, twenty-first-century merchandise which seems out of place for a play written when the word 'mouse' had only one meaning.

It's hardly surprising it should all feel so old-fashioned. It's an entertainment, after all, of the 1940s, which was born when Queen Mary asked the BBC for 'a new Agatha Christie' (the prolific author was a royal favourite) to mark her eightieth birthday. Those were the days when monarchs spake and subjects curtseyed. The writer obliged with a 30-minute radio play called *Three Blind Mice*. Nothing more might have been heard of it, but Christie, who called herself 'a perfect sausage machine', decided to add extra characters and created a stage play, which runs for almost exactly two hours.

The Mousetrap opened in Nottingham in October 1952 and briefly toured the Midlands and the north of England before settling into the Ambassador Theatre in the West End on November 25. It transferred to the larger St Martin's Theatre next door on March 25, 1974.

No one, least of all Christie, imagined such success. Five of her plays and another based on her novel had been staged and some had flopped. The most recent, *The Hollow*, had enjoyed a run of 376 performances, but Christie doubted *The Mousetrap* would last more than six months.

Her instinct was wrong, but not far wrong: for two years, with husband and wife Richard Attenborough and Sheila Sim in main roles, the show prospered. But when they left in 1955, the box office plummeted. The theatre even gave the production notice to quit.

What happened next has been called the Mousetrap Effect, though it's a phenomenon familiar to any show biz types who have seen the way a buzz can rescue a dying show or turn a slight success into a blockbuster. News of the imminent closure boosted ticket sales as people crowded to catch a performance. Success built on failure and then on success. The rest, as they say, is history.

In the twenty-first century – and now comfortably into its second half-century – *The Mousetrap* has become a sort of theatrical *perpetuum mobile*, whose longevity any dispassionate assessment struggles to explain. Christie herself would remark years later that the play had 'a bit of something in it for almost everybody' (though it's hard to see what it has in it for modern audiences reared on detectives like Morse or Rebus or drama like *The Silence of the Lambs*). It has become a cultural paradox, an ageless anachronism. Why it should have so outperformed, for example, *Witness for the Prosecution* – which opened a year later and ran 468 performances in London before moving to New York for an even longer run – remains the play's real mystery.

No one could be happier about the play's success than the writer's only grandson, Mathew Prichard, who was nine years old when it was written. When Christie handed to producer Peter Saunders in early 1952 a package of pages with the words 'This is a little present for you', it was really a present for the boy: she had already arranged to leave the play and its proceeds in trust for him.

It turned out to be young Mathew's lucky day. The West End takings are well over $100 million, never mind the royalties from other productions. As an act of generosity, if not philanthropy, it rivals J. M. Barrie's gift of *Peter Pan* to the Great Ormond Street Hospital for Sick Children (the hospital still banks the Disney cheques from time to time) and Handel's donation of the *Messiah* to a hospital for foundlings.

Spare a thought, by contrast, for John Woolf, a producer who bought the film rights in the mid-fifties. A clause in the contract provided that no film may be released for six months after the play's final performance – a restriction designed to protect the play's advantage of surprise about who actually did 'done' it. Woolf was plainly no slouch at picking a winner – his credits include *The African Queen* and *The Day of the Jackal* – but he died in 1999 without having had the chance to exercise his option.

The pub is called the Three Greyhounds, and although it is crowded we find a man sitting alone at a four-person table and ask if we might share it. He eyes us a trifle anxiously I fancy; he is waiting for someone, he says, and he plainly isn't sure that our arrival is conducive to a successful assignation. But he nods and I wave Mum to her seat. She has barely landed in it before she announces that 'We've come all the way from New Zealand and this is my first pub.'

Our tablemate, a suave Frenchman who speaks impeccable English, is taking a sip of beer at the time, and the combination of gasp and snort with which he greets this news violently irrigates his sinus cavities with best bitter. The liquid then exits in a fine spray, which lightly mists the fine wool fabric of his elegant suit.

'You don't say,' he says at last, mopping himself down with a silk handkerchief. Dimly it occurs to me that the phrase is quaintly antique, something that Betty Grable might say. Perhaps she was his English tutor on afternoon re-runs of Hollywood classics. I ask Mum what she wants to drink.

'Oh, gawn,' she says sounding like an amalgam of characters from her beloved *Coronation Street*, 'I'll 'ave an 'arf.'

I muscle my way to the bar and return laden with a pint and a half to find Mother earnestly engaged in conversation with the tablemate.

' … soooo expensive!' she is saying, eyeing the blackboard menu.

'There's a place next door that sells all you can eat for £3.50,' replies the Frenchman, flashing me a pitiably supplicant look. I pretend not to notice.

'No, this'll be fine,' I say. I've spotted the Chinese takeaway on the way in, where rows of bains-marie under lights act as incubators of salmonella and more dangerous diseases. I settle down over my pint. Shortly, the Frenchman leaves. He says his friend isn't coming any more, but I am left with the distinct impression that he's decided it will be safer to wait in the middle of the road.

We both choose the 'Scottish steak and ale pie', which comes with the universal accompaniment of chips and peas. Mum falls upon it as though it were the finest cuisine, sighing with pleasure at every mouthful. I enjoy the extra space created by the departure of the beer-sprayed Frenchman.

The food, and Mum's love of it, is the first clear sign of her Englishness. I find it mostly loathsome though oddly familiar. I was raised on this food: steak and kidney pies, big fatty roast meals, fresh vegetables boiled to mush-point.

It was the diet of Englishmen that had been transplanted into the countryside of the colonies. But though the style was reminiscent of the old country, the similarity ended there; in quality and quantity the fat of this land and that one were a world apart. In England mutton was a luxury; in New Zealand spring lamb was a birthright. Men ate four kinds of meat for breakfast before bending their backs to the shearing or scaling hillsides with a sheaf of half-round fence posts seesawing across muscled shoulders.

In town – which is what Hamilton was when I was growing up in it – we were fattened on the menus of our forebears: corned beef and cabbage, pickled pork, dumplings and suet, and bread-and-butter pudding. This was the diet of coal miners and navvies and dockworkers in the gloomy, grey industrial towns of a land on the other side of the world.

Of course we could eat better. London, in particular Soho, where we are sitting, is rich in eateries, ethnic, trendy or gimmicky (one, called Garlic, uses that aromatic bulb in everything including its desserts). But I have learnt to be cautious about taking Mum to eat ethnic, and particularly spicy, food given her propensity for fainting when she does. So we plough through the 'steak pie' and I have another pint and I sigh and stare at the people walking past and wonder at how we've come halfway around the world to a place that tastes remarkably like home.

Actually, of course, home tasted of England. These days New Zealand cuisine, which exploits our fresh produce and, in particular, the fabulous seafood, is distinctive and delicious, full of clean and simple flavours. Perversely, just as our own cuisine comes of age, the better-heeled and more discerning of the New Zealand restaurant-going public look elsewhere – principally to Europe and Asia – for their gastronomic thrills. Cookery books are full of recipes calling for Arborio rice or Turkish breads or arcane pasta and pesto or shiitake mushrooms or lemongrass. We are directed to Asian supermarkets or specialist food importers for the ingredients.

To some extent it's a result of supply creating demand: the nineties' wave of immigration has hugely enriched our ethnic composition and the menus available to the adventurous diner. Yet I can't help wondering if it's a version of the famous cultural cringe as well, which assumes that something from afar is better than our own.

In the days when Mum cooked everything I ate, she cooked according to a recipe book in her head, one given to her by her mother before her. The wife of a Yorkshireman and a widow of the Depression, Nana always cooked for appetites created on the other side of the world and her daughter learnt to do the same. It was almost as if, to paraphrase Gertrude Stein's famous remark about San Francisco, 'There was no here here.'

So we grew up on roast beef and Yorkshire pudding, on Cornish pasties (much tastier, as I was soon to find, than the ones they make in Cornwall), and on steak and kidney pudding – not pie; the soggy, stodgy topping was made not with butter-rich pastry but with dumplings, which called for the more economical beef dripping.

In part, of course, this was a result of a poverty mentality created by the Depression and the war, when butter was rationed. But in the late fifties and early sixties when these meals were cooked, New Zealand was prosperous and so were we. So it was more than domestic economy that dictated what landed on the dinner table. We ate as we lived, like Englishmen.

One Christmas dinner we dined on quail – one each – and Dad sat proudly at the head of the table. Looking back, I fancy he was revelling in the sense that he was an English squire. In my memory, he is in waistcoat and white shirt, hardly suitable garb for a New Zealand Christmas, but he would have been just back from church and that was what he wore, winter and summer. Maybe the image is of him on another Sunday. But he is evidently delighted at the notion that we are eating quail. We four boys wonder at the palatability of a shrivelled, bony bird which we have to eat carefully, like fish, so we don't chew down on the bits of lead shot that are scattered through the scanty meat. We pine for a turkey. Yet even Christmas turkey seems odd in the sweltering heat of a New Zealand summer.

We were not alone in this of course. The story of being raised as an Englishman in a land as far as may be found from England is the story of my generation. And just as we were fed stories of Drake's triumph over the Armada and the glory that was London during the Blitz, we were fed the food that little Englishmen ate. When I finally rebelled in the mid-eighties and insisted that Christmas dinner should be barbecues and salads and fresh fish and fruits, Mum saw it as a kind of treachery, the betrayal of a tradition to which I ought to have shown greater respect.

We've been warned to arrive early at the Abbey. The middle of August is still the height of the tourist season and Mum's hip is not up to standing in queues. So we're there by 8 a.m., only to find it doesn't open until 9 a.m. and the yard outside the east door where tourists form two orderly lines is empty. I don't want to waste our early arrival so I sit cross-legged on the cobbles, reading the papers in a queue of one, while Mum perches uncomfortably on a ledge at the base of a wall.

It isn't long before an attendant spots her and helpfully fetches a chair so she can sit in some comfort under a nearby tree while I hold our place. Within a few minutes the queue is stretching out into the street. My position allows me a good vantage point from which to observe the idiotic questions staff at tourist attractions have to endure. I lose count of the number who stroll up to the front of the queue to ask the attendant: a) whether this is Westminster Abbey; (b) whether this is the real one, where the coronations take place; c) whether this is where you are meant to queue; d) what time the Abbey opens (this question is usually posed immediately after a lengthy perusal of the sign, which lists the opening hours in large letters), and so on. These questions are invariably answered with an astonishingly good-natured courtesy by men who plainly have to endure them dozens of times daily.

Once inside, I seat Mum in the wheelchair that has been fetched for her and we pick up a couple of audio guides. The 'hands-free' kit they had at the Cabinet War Rooms has not, alas, occurred to the good folks at Westminster Abbey; so I am forced to push the wheelchair while cocking my head at a deformed angle and cradling the audio guide against my shoulder. This means any writing – inscriptions on plaques and tombstones, say, with which the Abbey positively teems – looks as though it is in the Cyrillic alphabet. Other visitors, plainly thinking I am some sort of hunchback, scurry past, which affords them some protection from what happens when I try to hold the guide with one hand and push the wheelchair with the other.

Lopsidedly propelled, the chair roams in circles like a ride-on mower whose owner has expired mid-lawn. Mum, dizzy with the loopy movement, finds herself repeatedly heading for somewhere she has just been. This is not something she takes to kindly. Indeed she loudly proclaims my failings as a driver, her voice bouncing off the ancient tombs and the Gothic arches of the roof, until I bring the chair under control.

Of everything on show at the Abbey, it is the Coronation Chair, the great throne on which every English monarch has sat to be crowned since the late thirteenth century, which I find most remarkable. It is not for its majesty – you can find more impressive chairs in any design store and it's as tatty as you'd expect any 700-year-old piece of furniture to be – but what is most striking is the graffiti that covers every part of its surface.

Most of it, the stuff on the back out of view of the passing tourist, is the work of the boys of Westminster School who carved their names with pride in the eighteenth and nineteenth centuries. But many marks are the work of much more modern tourists. I have heard more than once that such inspiring exhortations as 'Smoke more dope' and 'Karen loves Billy' are to be found engraved in the ancient wood. These days you can't get close enough to find out, but the decision to protect a chair that is so central to the idea of the British monarchy is extraordinarily recent. The Chapel of St Edward the Confessor, where the chair sat for 700 years, was open to general visitors until 1997; it was only in February 1998 that it was raised onto a modern pedestal out of reach of tourists armed with Swiss army knives and the determination to make their mark on history.

We move around the Abbey's edge and I take the opportunity to plant another kiss on the foot of the life-size likeness of Shakespeare in Poet's Corner. At the front of the nave I show Mum where the chair would have been placed for the coronation in 1953 and where the Queen Mother's coffin would have sat in the most recent state occasion. She emits a longing, loyal sigh and gazes about her as though inhaling the atmosphere. As she plods up the aisle, backlit in the dusty air, she looks small and frail and happy.

I recall her ambition 'just to walk where the Queen has trod', which I had seen as so silly when she'd first mentioned it. But watching her walk down the aisle past the choir, I can almost see the fanfare exploding in her old grey head and imagine her kneeling before her monarch who thanks her for a lifetime of devotion and loyalty. For a long instant, as she lights a candle at the Tomb of the Unknown Soldier, I see her ambition for this trip coalescing into this single instant when a royalist's pilgrimage comes to an end. It fills me with pride as well as a sort of sadness.

It is part of ageing, I suppose, that you can – indeed, you need to – contemplate the possibility that some things you do you will never do again. We never dream it when we are young, being consumed in the endless present and in our power in it. But in this moment I know, as Mum does, that she will not pass this way again. Here is the point at which she will turn for home.

I want to leave her there, in a way, to have her die at the moment of an epiphany. But we have more practical objectives to achieve.

We have a cup of tea on a park bench outside as a wild-eyed Irishman with tobacco-stained teeth moves through the crowd bellowing at each person in turn and brandishing a fistful of unwritten postcards.

'You haven't got any stamps have you stamps,' he chants, the utterance unpunctuated but inflected with an oddly charming musicality. Most turn away from him. Anything Irish has an uncomfortable resonance in a city where they've mostly removed the public rubbish bins to stop them being used to conceal bombs.

We make our way down the river to the Tower. Along the way I point out Cleopatra's Needle. It was a gift from the Viceroy of Egypt to the people of Britain in 1819 as 'a worthy memorial' to Nelson's victory over the French in the Battle of the Nile, and it was not erected on this spot for another 60 years. The inscriptions make it plain that it had nothing to do with the fabled queen of Alexandria at all; it was carved from stone quarried 1500 years before she was around and erected by the Romans in that city almost 20 years after the good lady had made the fatal decision to suckle a poisonous snake.

Pictures taken at the time it was erected on the Thames Embankment make it look impressive, but it is now dwarfed by the line of trees among which it hides and can only be seen from the river or when you're standing under it.

'It's very small,' says Mum, which has become something of a refrain for her. I breathe deeply and lean towards her.

'We're going to come to the Globe in a minute, Mum, which was built expressly to stage the plays of a good mate of mine. If you say that it's small, I shall throw you in the river. It may not look much alongside the shopping centre at Whangaparaoa, but it was pretty impressive when they knocked it up and anyway, size isn't everything.'

She laughs as the thatched and plastered shape of Shakespeare's Globe comes into view.

This is a replica, of course. The original Globe burnt down in 1613 during a performance of *Henry V*, and was immediately rebuilt with a roof of tiles, not flammable thatch. It was, like all playhouses in London, closed by the Puritans in 1642 and – in an astonishingly modern gesture – pulled down to make way for tenements two years later. The reconstruction, the dream of American-born actor Sam Wanamaker, opened in 1997. Although Wanamaker worked tirelessly on the project from 1970, he died in 1993 and never saw the fruits of his work.

We disembark at Tower Pier and look for a place to eat lunch. All the riverside park benches are occupied, so I take Mum into a shady courtyard restaurant and ask the waitress whether we can eat our sandwiches there if we buy a cup of tea.

'You don't 'ave to buy nuffing,' she says cheerily and unhesitatingly. I would attribute her generosity to sympathy for my elderly companion but Mum's seated some distance away when I ask and it seems it's part of a relaxed policy. It would be unthinkable in New Zealand, where proprietors of cafés will at least glower and probably evict you bodily for eating your own food at their tables, even if you buy a cuppa from them.

The entrance to the Tower is several hundred long, limping metres away from the pier and the summer heat, which has made its presence felt throughout our visit, is now hammering. I find Mum a spot where she can sit in the shade while I queue for half an hour. But as soon as we get inside I begin wondering whether it was a good idea. The crowds are thickly clustered around anything of interest, including the Beefeaters who act as guides, and any sense of history evaporates in the blistering heat.

I do get the chance to pause contemplatively at the Traitors' Gate, where boatmen brought the condemned on their last journey. It's walled off from the river now, but the low arch and the baleful water-level portcullis are still plainly visible from the inside. I imagine the gate opening to admit Thomas More, the 'man for all seasons' of Robert Bolt's play, who went to the scaffold rather than make the simple and expedient declaration of something he didn't believe in.

The Tower was built in the eleventh century, which was a bit before allowing for wheelchair access became a requirement of town planning applications. Certainly any plan I might have to push Mum around here is quickly abandoned. The place is full of flights of steps and stairs, most of them hidden under the human tide of tourists slowly flowing forwards. Mum is uncomfortable and sore-legged and I know how she feels, but we join the shuffle up narrow spiral staircases not recommended for those given to claustrophobia.

Through rooms of armour and swords and flags we troop, though I'm now so tired they just look like a lot of old stuff. At last we reach the Crown Jewels and I'm interested to see that they are not just the orb and sceptre and big crown from the coronation but a huge array of different regalia. It takes several long minutes just to walk past it.

It's late and we're tired. We make it back up to Tower Hill Gate just opposite the tube station. The bus stop to the east seems distant in the heat, way back by the bridge, so I head west in search of the next stop, which I assume will be closer. Mum follows a dozen limping paces behind. Heading west turns out to be a serious blunder, but by the time that becomes obvious we've reached a point where going back seems even less attractive than plugging on. We are walking along a windy tunnel of arterial road, along the backs of buildings that are plainly riverfront. I can see no easy way to penetrate the wall, and the road snarls with cars and buses displaying distressingly familiar route numbers. Every hundred metres takes us no closer to our goal.

'I think we should get a taxi,' I tell Mum.

'We'll do no such thing,' she splutters, panting and perspiring heavily as she leans on her stick.

I gaze ahead. The road, looking like an urban landscape out of *Blade Runner*, seems to go on to the vanishing point and the cars speeding past so fast they make my fillings rattle are plainly enjoying being on a stretch of roadway where there is never any reason to stop. I figure we are more likely to find a leprechaun than a bus stop.

'We'll get there,' Mum's saying. 'Just keep going.'

Gloomily I plough on, with Mum thump-clicking behind me on her fold-up walking stick.

We were raised to fear spending money. Bill Bryson, in *The Lost Continent: Travels in Small Town America* wrote of his father's determination on family holidays to cook dinner on the roadside on his portable gas stove rather than take them 'some place with air-conditioning, linen tablecloths and ice cubes clinking in glasses of clear water'.

'He wouldn't have it,' Bryson concluded. 'He was a child of the Depression and where capital outlays were involved he always wore the haunted look of a fugitive who had just heard bloodhounds in the distance.'

When I first read that passage, I laughed until the tears rolled freely, but it was the slightly bitter laugh of recognition.

My mother was a child of the Depression, too, and it was a worse Depression for her than for many because she had no father and her mother was constantly anxious about money. Even a hint of extravagance was frowned on, and waste was virtually criminal. On our first morning in London I had gone shopping for milk and tea and other essentials for the flat.

'Get me some muesli,' she had said. 'And a pawpaw would be nice to go with it.'

I walked miles looking for a pawpaw and finally, just before I was going to give up, ran one down in the Berwick Street market only a couple of hundred yards from the apartment. I held one aloft. It was barely larger than a cricket ball.

'A pahnd each, sir,' the barrow boy told me.

I took it and delivered it. It festered slowly on the bench for the next three days and I made to throw it out as we were packing to leave. But Mum wouldn't hear of it. She packed it up, renewing her promise to eat it and by the time she took it out, on our first morning in the south-west, it was a mangled pulpy thing. But she insisted on dissecting it and rescuing the few edible morsels with a teaspoon, forcing a mouthful on me and staring imperiously as she dared me to say it wasn't delicious.

'Fuck this,' I say, turning and walking backwards and trailing my outstretched arm in the stream of traffic.

'What are you doing?' Mum demands. She looks close to collapse.

'Going home,' I reply as a taxi pulls up. I jerk open the door and heave her in. She protests feebly and I can see her fretting all the way back as the meter ticks up to £13.60.

'Enjoy it, Mum,' I say, as much for my own benefit as hers. 'You've earned it.'

'There was no need for such extravagance,' she says. 'We were almost there.'

She may be right. I make a point of not asking the driver about how far it would have been if we had kept walking. Best not to know these things.

WIDOWS' MIGHT

When Mum's father died on October 13, 1925, his widow faced a harsh reality. Her widow's pension paid only 2s 6d per week per child, not enough to provide for the upbringing of her children, much less her own needs. She had to make plans for a stable income. In doing so, she turned to her past for inspiration.

Widowhood and penury were something of a family tradition. Nana's mother, Rose, had been widowed early; her husband, Charlie, had died in 1899 at only 45 when Nana was barely 13, the third of six children ranging in age from six to sixteen. My uncle Geoff's family history notes only that Charlie succumbed to 'a liver complaint', which may be suggestive of the taste for liquor.

But the first Whites to live and die in New Zealand, the descendants of Henry and Priscilla whose trail I had followed in Cornwall, were similarly struck by the tragedy of a father's early death. Charlie was one of Henry and Priscilla's nine children – two, born in the West Country, had arrived on the *Westminster* with them – and Henry's early end was recorded in the *New Zealand Herald* of July 20, 1868 under the poetic heading 'Melancholy Death of Mr Henry White'.

On the previous morning, the report read, 'Some persons walking on the Queen Street Wharf observed an object floating in the water. The Police boat, which was just shoving off from the Watermen's Stairs, was hailed. Upon raising it into the boat, it was quickly recognised as the body of Mr Henry White, the well-known contractor and builder of this city. The Police boat immediately conveyed its melancholy burden to the deadhouse in Official Bay.'

It's hard to escape the conclusion that liquor played its part in this death, too. Henry had been seen the previous afternoon 'in good spirits', the coroner was later told, a phrase that did not then carry the double entendre with which it is loaded today. Just before midnight he had knocked on the door of a hotel in

Victoria Street and, the publican told the Coroner's Court, asked to be allowed to 'rest awhile'.

'But he did not seek a bed,' Geoff writes, 'and was refused admission as it was after hours.'

If the coroner thought to ask whether Mr White was the worse for liquor, the answer is not recorded. But the fact that he was 'refused admission' is instructive, since it suggests he sought it and seeking admission to a bar that has already closed is not typically the act of an entirely sober man.

In Auckland, barely a quarter century after the *Westminster* docked, reputation was an important commodity, and protecting the sensibilities of the bereaved must have played a large part in the conduct of judicial proceedings. Geoff protests too much, perhaps, when he notes that Henry's 'good reputation was well established'; Mum doesn't like the suggestion, but I can't help wondering whether it was actually well protected.

Henry was meant to have met his 14-year-old son, Charles – my mother's grandfather – off a steamer from Thames expected around midnight. 'He must have missed his footing and been unable to save himself,' Geoff concludes. 'The wharf was not well lit and it was a dark, stormy night.'

But he also speculates that Henry 'must by then have been very tired'. This reads as a bleakly comic observation in a world where the satirical British magazine *Private Eye*'s use of the term 'tired and emotional' to mean imprudently drunk has passed into common usage.

Certainly Henry was held in high esteem. He was publicly described in later years by one of his building associates as 'a highly esteemed citizen of early Auckland and no better proof of his sterling character could be adduced than the deep regard in which he was held by his workmen'. Much of his legacy has been demolished now – as has much of the inner city – before the wrecking ball that swung through the reckless 1980s. But some remains: the Methodist Church in Pitt Street; the Customhouse; and what the *Herald* at the time of his death called 'the Lunatic Asylum' – Oakley and later Carrington Hospital, which is now mostly given over to a polytech. Most visible in contemporary photographs of Auckland is Partington's

Mill, which loomed on the uptown ridge until 1950.

It seems a sad and sordid end for a man who had achieved such status in his new home, to be found floating face down at the edge of the harbour. Reading the report now, I can't help visually connecting the Watermen's Stairs and the Mayflower Steps. Henry, having embarked on that brave journey and having made a go of it in this small southern land, died like one who has failed to make the leap across the expanse of water from the arriving boat. Perhaps, at the last minute, he was drawn back to the water that had borne him here, wondering – like any immigrant, and like me – how it might have been if he had never come at all.

Henry's success in business left Priscilla well provided for and in any case she had adult children to care for her, but Rose did not. She took in boarders in her rented terrace house at 5 Dilworth Terrace, Parnell – now restored to gentrified splendour after a period as a virtual slum. One of them was Francis Edward Buckley, a 21-year-old Yorkshireman fresh off the boat.

Thus, writes Geoff, 'My parents were thrown together and soon formed an attachment,' which would last until suddenly severed by a single gunshot in the pre-dawn darkness of a Papatoetoe orchard in 1925.

Geoff, who wrote his family memoir after a lifetime of labour with the National Insurance Company, cannot resist gently chiding his long-dead father for not having insured his life.

'His father had opposed this form of investment, describing it as gambling,' Geoff writes. He forbears to note that this attitude – not to mention the son's adoption of it – was more than a little imprudent, given the history of death and widowhood on the maternal side of the family. But the observation he does make befits a lifelong insurance salesman.

'Even a small policy would have helped mother's problems and it was so nearly a position she reached. A life insurance agent had called on her several times offering an "industrial" policy for a shilling or two per week [but] mother was very afraid of Frank's objection.'

Thus unprovided for, Nana looked to provide for herself. For two years after Frank's death, she battled on at Papatoetoe, occasionally taking the long train trip into the city to seek advice from businessmen, friends of the family, as to how she might secure her future. When a small shop became vacant on the corner of Vulcan Lane and High Street, Nana mulled over the idea of starting tearooms.

Her baking skills were certainly up to it. From a cloud of flour and a knob of butter she could conjure a batch of fluffy light scones and slip them into the oven on a dusted tray in little more time than it takes to say so in writing. It was an afternoon speciality guaranteed to capture the fancy of hungry grandsons, and my playmates and I devoured the results, sitting sticky-fingered and butter-chinned on the back steps. We would scamper away still chewing our last mouthfuls, with never a thought to thank her.

Baking was an activity as natural, as autonomic as breathing. I was always enthralled to watch as she mixed a cake. She would twist free the stainless-steel bowl of Mum's Kenwood Chef cake mixer – an appliance she derided as a new-fangled frippery – and measure the ingredients into the bowl in handfuls. (I once asked her for a recipe, but its quantities were all expressed as 'a bit' of this, 'a little bit' of that and 'a couple' of something else.) The same hands would mix and stir and knead and pound, and only at particularly soggy stages of the procedure would she relent and resort to the technology of a wooden spoon.

So she didn't lack the skills or will to start the city tearooms, and might have even been persuaded to invest in a cake mixer, but she lacked the money. The banks in those days were not keen on lending to a solo woman. Well-heeled old friends, among them Frank's former employers, offered to back her, but she was afraid of the level of debt she would have had to assume to start such a business and of what she would do if it failed.

At last she decided to take in boarders, as her mother had done before her. She had expected to keep house her whole life and it was all she knew how to do. The man for whom she had planned to care had killed himself, so what she once had planned to do for love she would now do for money. The time it took her to reach that conclusion hints at an understandable reluctance. She must have known that she was condemning herself to a life of unremitting toil, but at least she would have realised that she would be providing a home for her children at the same time.

She rented a large house in Ranfurly Road, Epsom, alongside the small park on the corner of Manukau Road. Part of it was originally built as the stables for the residence of the owner, a city merchant who lived a couple of doors up the street. She cleaned it up and advertised for 'paying guests', a term she preferred to 'boarder' since it lent some tone to the establishment she was trying to create.

'Mother worried a great deal about getting replies to her first advertisements,' Geoff writes. 'It was, she feared, "so far out of town". Would people travel all that way, pay the fourpence required for the long three sections on the Onehunga tram to reach work in the city?

'She worried unnecessarily. She soon had the place full.'

Much later, a small boy sits up in bed, his eyes wide in his freckled face, listening to a bedtime story. His father, a doctor, has just set up in private practice in the town. Still unable to afford rooms – still unsure whether he can make sufficient success of the practice to justify such an expense – he consults in the master bedroom and the three boys are crammed in together to free up a bedroom for Mum and Dad.

He has advertised in the newspaper, too, but the patients, who are slow to respond to the presence of a new doctor in their midst, are staying away in droves. The doctor has given up a comfortable salaried job in a power project town in the South Waikato to start afresh here and has shouldered a £3000 mortgage to buy this £5000 house.

The boy, not yet four, is too young to understand the anxiety that attends on the establishment of a new business. For the adults, that anxiety is an ache in the pit of the stomach, a nagging sensory backdrop to the most banal daily tasks. But even if the significance eludes him, the boy knows, with the exquisite certainty of which only the very young are capable, what the parents keep talking about, what they long for.

The storyteller father gets to the point in the story where the three bears have left for their picnic.

'And then,' he says, with a dramatic flourish, 'who should this be, walking up the path? Who do you think it is?'

'A patient,' I say.

Like Dad's patients, Nana's 'paying guests' soon turned up. For between £1 and 30s a week, they got full board: a cooked breakfast, a cut lunch (cooked on weekends) and dinner, and fresh linen each week. For Nana it meant endless drudgery, from 6 a.m. to 10 p.m. most days. On Saturdays, she would stoke the firebox beneath the brick-clad copper to do the laundry – including the bed linen and work clothes of eight adults – by hand.

Mum recalls coming home and finding her mother 'polishing the floor and crying her heart out', but I seldom saw Nana cry. Stoicism was her strong suit, even in the face of the resentful sarcasm with which my father often lashed her. He sometimes reduced her to something close to tears, but she bit them back. She cried at my young brother's baptism, but my parents told me that she always cried in church. That was why she never went, they said, although I fancy it had more to do with the fact that she did not – could not – believe in a kind and loving God. In church, she knew that she was in the presence of a God who had meted out to her the punishment of a bad fortune she had never deserved.

But if I never saw her cry, I never saw her smile either. When she sat at our dining table, she seemed always to be striving to make herself inconspicuous, to shrink into the background of a family where she always felt like a guest. Loss was more than a part of her life; it was her identity. She *was* her loss, and her life was something lived in its gloomy shadow.

When I told Mum this, she looked sad and disputed my memory. She reminded me of how Nana would appear at the lounge door dressed up as Santa Claus to dispense largesse on Christmas morning. The deception fooled none of us. Nana, a tiny, frail figure of about 8 stone, bore not even a passing resemblance to a big, florid Santa, and the high-pitched clucking emanating from behind the clouds of surgical cotton wool inexpertly attached to her face – which reminded me of nothing so much as the chooks who pecked in the shade of the orchard – was as far as might be imagined from the cheerful, booming 'Ho! Ho! Ho!' of the authentic Santa. But we were smart enough to play along because we wanted the contents of the pillowcase she bore. Years later, I heard the British raconteur Sir Peter Ustinov say that he never believed in Santa Claus but he went along with the fiction because he thought his parents did and that pretty much nailed it.

So Nana's life was one of ceaseless toil. It also meant living with permanent, if small, debts – mainly to the grocer and butcher. Each week she would pile the guests' payments on the table and make piles for each creditor, to ensure that her creditworthiness – and, more importantly, her dignity – was preserved.

When, years later, she left the house and moved on to the next stage of her life, keeping home for a farmer in Drury, she still owed the grocer £20 – about $400 in twenty-first-century money; he told her to forget it.

This sort of upbringing prepared Mum for the early years of married life. My eldest brother was born while Dad was in the second year of his medical training in Dunedin and their entire income was a returned serviceman's bursary of £5 a week. Even when they came back to Auckland when Dad was in his house surgeon's year at Auckland Hospital and they were living in a fibrolite bungalow behind Dad's parents' house in Park Road almost opposite the Domain Gates, money was tight. Mum would often tell us as we grew up how she divided their meagre income between tins – one for groceries, one for meat, one for bread and so on – and spent only what she had. One tin was labelled 'Entertainment', and when the contents amounted to something worth spending it would more often go on sheet music than a night at the pictures.

I would come back to live at that same fibro house in my student years, long after my grandparents died, when it was still owned by Dad and his brother and administered by the Public Trustee. It was a dark, damp hole and the beautiful garden Mum had made in front of the bungalow was reduced to long grass. Castor oil plants sprouted shrub-size from the brick-walled beds either side of the steps leading up to the front verandah.

The state of the grounds infuriated the neighbour, a veteran of the British Army whose tonsured lawns and precisely ordered gardens were insulted by the mess over the fence. But the rent was cheap and while our circumstances, on student incomes, may have seemed straitened, I never thought of myself as poor. This was the privileged late sixties; mine was a lifestyle choice of fashionable bohemianism.

For Mum, enforced poverty – or something close to it – was a constant companion in the last third of her life. She had worked hard – the way women of her generation did – being a wife and mother while Dad built up his medical practice and for less than 20 years from the mid-1950s, she knew something approaching affluence. Then, with three of the four boys having left home, Dad abruptly left her.

She left Hamilton soon after, perhaps driven by the shamed sense of having failed at the only task she had set herself in life. She re-established herself at Manly on the Whangaparaoa Peninsula, north of Auckland, when that was a landscape of seaside villages separated by rolling fields, and set herself to seeing her youngest son through school.

Dad remarried and lived in the affluence his status in the city demanded – a new car every couple of years, overseas trips. Meanwhile Mum counted the pennies at Manly and worked in the opportunity shop of her local church, keeping her eyes peeled for bargains – a battered toaster, a serviceable pair of shoes – for herself or us.

It was not exactly poverty but it was a greater imperative to be careful with money than one might expect a doctor's wife to have to answer. Yet looking back, I realise that it was more than just a process of adapting to the misfortune of circumstance. In pursuing a life of grinding frugality, Mum was only doing what all the mothers of her generation had learnt early to do. And she was also answering the call of her genetic inheritance – an innate sense of the need for economy.

I am often conscious that – in material terms at least – I grew up in the most privileged time and place in the history of the planet. Plenty of people have been more wealthy, but they have lived in countries or eras characterised by cruel or criminal divides between the rich and the poor. New Zealand – and more specifically Hamilton – in the 1950s was a time and place of plenty and by the time I was old enough to care about how much money my parents had, they had plenty.

Yet even when Dad's medical practice was firing and Mum could afford to buy the best cuts, we ate them sparingly. Liver in rich gravy might be sweetened with a rasher of bacon, but neck chops and oxtails rumbled for whole afternoons in pressure-cooked stews on the stovetop.

In a sense, of course, that kind of cuisine was not driven exclusively by the urge to economise. It was an expression of who Mum was, the enunciation of an idea of home and home-maker that was completely in tune with the time. Recipes appear in modern glossy magazines accompanying articles about 'slow food'. It's a revolt against fast food, but really it's just food the way it used to be before mothers stopped staying home and cooking. The so-called 'slow food movement' reveals a modern hankering for those days when dinner was not something eaten from a polystyrene pack or transferred from supermarket freezer to microwave oven. Mum's long, laboured cooking was an expression of herself; she loved us, as filmmaker Peter Wells said of his own mother in the film *Pansy*, by nourishing us.

I knew from an early age what bought biscuits were. Indeed I first contemplated the concept of infinity as I looked at a Bycroft tin on the bottom shelf at the grocers. The large container, as big as a kerosene tin, from which the grocer would fill small bags for retailing, had on its label a picture of a running boy holding under his arm a tin with a label with a picture of a running boy holding under his arm … I can't remember eating bought biscuits except at other people's places. Mum would never have dreamt of buying biscuits, yet the biscuit tins were always full. In our house in the middle of the world's richest dairy country, butter-rich baking was a weekly duty at least – chocolate squares sprinkled with a snowstorm of desiccated coconut, and shortbread crimped with workaday thumbs into hourglass shapes that proclaimed their home-made status.

No doubt there were times when she might have added some fancy confection to the grocery list. But to do so would have been to betray her very reason for being. What's more, there remained a sense that enjoying the ability to spend money – not even engaging in wild extravagance, but simply relaxing in the knowledge that, for the first time in the life of the family, more money was coming in than was going out – was a form of foolhardiness, a tempting of fate. When she did serve fillet steak, the helpings were always small, as though she felt guilty about living in relative ease and conscious always that hard times were not far behind and not far ahead.

Buffeted by these mixed messages, it is little wonder that I showed an early predilection for juvenile delinquency. I blame – because I can – a schoolmate called Gert. He was the son of Danish immigrants and he endured the constant taunt that his name was short for Gertrude. He didn't look very feminine to me, but he looked pretty funny because he wore knee-length knickerbockers and long plaid socks and stout sensible shoes that looked like mountaineer's boots.

But I realised he had hidden talent when we stopped on the way home one day at the corner shop so I could spend the two pennies I had on 10 aniseed balls. I didn't like aniseed balls especially but I bought them because they were five for a penny and when it came to buying lollies on the way home from school, quantity was everything.

I have no idea where I got the tuppence – I don't think pocket money was a concept that had penetrated my parents' consciousness at that time – but it was a rare event that I had the money to spend.

Mr Rice carefully counted out my 10 aniseed balls into a paper bag. I handed over my two pennies. Then Gert stepped forward and placed his order.

He asked for a bag of mixed jubes so large that it was only just measurable in ounces rather than pounds. I had only seen such monsters at weddings and twenty-first birthdays where they were provided to extract the co-operative silence of a legion of unruly kids. Gert plainly intended to devour them alone.

The bag was almost too large for him to hold in one hand; but he had to, because the other hand was taken up with a quarter-gallon bottle of fizzy drink of a colour as green as envy. It was an impressive display, beyond the power of a year's supply of tuppences to encompass, but it was what happened next that truly filled me with awe.

'Charge it up, please, Mr Rice,' Gert said. I had no idea what he meant but it was an incantation with apparently magic powers since it allowed him to leave, groaning under the weight of his purchases, without any money changing hands.

We stood around on the store's gravel forecourt for a while, I sucking tentatively on one of my aniseed balls while Gert scarfed whole handfuls of jubes and poured lime fizz down his throat, before we went our separate ways. I walked home deep in thought.

The next day, reaching Rice's Store, I padded along the coir runner that lined the aisle leading to the counter and asked for my tuppence-worth of aniseed balls. The bag was filled, twisted, closed, dropped with a crinkly clunk on the counter. I uttered the magic words and Mr Rice reached for his book to record in ballpoint copperplate, the beginning of my juvenile crime spree.

What followed seemed like an endless summer of pleasure and sugar-laden plenty, although the realities of small business credit control make it obvious that it lasted at most a calendar month. One day, as I accompanied Dad on his house calls, he swung the VW onto the gravel forecourt outside the store. I stayed in the car, somewhat puzzled, as he walked inside; Dad after all, never shopped and I couldn't understand why he was stopping here now.

I did not have long to wait for an explanation. He disappeared into the dim interior of the shop for only a moment before noticing I wasn't creeping like a snail unwillingly in his wake. He poked his head out.

'Come on,' he said with some impatience. Puzzlement gave way to apprehension.

The inquisition took place in the back of the shop, where I was astonished to discover the Rices maintained a perfect facsimile of a family home, right down to a fully-equipped kitchen and living room. Examination-in-chief was conducted by my father, whose only notes appeared to be a copy of the Rices' latest invoice. He held it aloft for dramatic emphasis as he asked such rhetorical questions as 'Two bobs' worth of peppermint creams?'.

I knew these were questions because they rose at the end to a slightly elevated interrogative pitch, but I had no idea what the answers were. The logical thing to say to 'Two bobs' worth of peppermint creams?' was 'Yes, please!' or at least 'Yeah, they were fabulous!' but by this time the prosecution case was reaching a crescendo and I was pretty sure that these were not the answers being adduced.

The numerical extent of my larceny remains engraved on my mind. The invoice was for £2/1s/10d, which, as those who cannot remember pre-decimal currency might need to be told, was a substantial sum. Eight years later, I would earn only four times that amount for a whole week's holiday work.

No evidence was offered in my defence, but if there had been an advocate to speak for me, he might have said that I meant no harm. This young boy, he might have claimed, cannot be condemned as a thief since he never knowingly stole anything. He simply acted as his upbringing had taught him to act, as one for whom plenty is a right, as one to whom scarcity is unknown. If anyone erred here, it was parents who raised him free of the fear of want, who taught him that he could always have whatever he needed.

If my parents thought the experience would cure me of the predilection for petty theft, they were wrong. Tarnished by my record, I was not entrusted with money for some time except when I was given a coin for the collection plate at church. But it didn't take me long to realise that the act of offertory was a private one, between me and the good Lord. In short, if I left home with sixpence and a big brown penny was all that landed in the plate, it would be subject to the divine equivalent of lawyer-client privilege.

A squeaking soprano in the front row of the choir, at some distance from my mother – who stood among the contraltos with her eyes reverently fixed on the altar – I was protected from detection. In any case, as the plate came past, I could disguise the denomination of my offering by passing the drapery of my surplice across it. A penny landed with the same pious clink as a shilling, as a florin, as the fortune contained in the ornately decorated coin we – loyally English – called half a crown.

The feasibility of this subterfuge having been established, I could spend fully five-sixths of the money that burnt a hole in my Sunday best (if halfpennies had not already been withdrawn from circulation, my embezzlement would have been greater) and still make the necessary token offering. I had never understood what need God had for money, but kids miss the point like that. I was meant to be buying salvation; I bought chewy, fruit-flavoured bars wrapped in waxy paper.

Then, one sunny Sunday, it all came crashing down. Emerging from the shop at which I had stopped en route to church (needless to say, I picked a route that took me nowhere near the watchful Mr Rice), I peeled the wrapper off one of my penny crimes. Then something made me look up. Dad's car was passing. Our eyes locked. My bowels melted. I raised a hand in a weak and sickly wave. He slowed, then accelerated away, the air intakes on his VW Beetle hissing and plinking.

I spent the morning in white-surpliced purgatory, snatching a glance from time to time at my father perched behind the organ, but unable to see him behind his music stand. As soon as the service was over, I biked home with legs blurring as the half-eaten sugar bar gathered lint in my trouser pocket and set about a pre-emptive act of atonement by mowing the lawns, which didn't need mowing.

This did not have the desired effect since my father when he returned home padded along the path to the back door, his change clinking in his pockets, and barely acknowledged my greeting, despite the fact that it was delivered fortissimo with an almost hysterical gusto.

Soon enough I was summoned. The arraignment was held in the master bedroom (my memory is that Mum was sick, though perhaps the image of her lying afflicted took root only in an imagination crazed by the guilt of betraying her).

The examination complete, the stuttering inadequate defence delivered, sentence was passed.

'Last time you stole from us,' Dad intoned. 'This time you stole from God.'

I don't remember taking that utterance seriously, but the next one made my heart stop. I would be required to make a full public confession before the entire congregation the next Sunday.

It was, it occurs to me now, a gesture typical of my father: an act of dramatic theatre that would illustrate not my penitence but his conscientiousness as a disciplinarian. In any event, nothing came of it. Perhaps he forgot, perhaps Mum prevailed on him to commute the sentence. I never dared ask. But I liked to think that Mum showed the quality of mercy, that she knew instinctively that, like Galileo, I needed only be shown the instruments of torture without having to feel their bite. That, after all, is what Mums are supposed to do.

It's our last night in London and we wander up Greek Street. I'm hungering to eat at one of the area's fabled restaurants – L'Escargot appeals; since Mum's paying, it won't matter that we get little change out of £100. But she is taken by an elderly Greek woman sitting at a doorway from which a staircase leads down. She stands as we inspect the menu on the door and with a sweeping bow, gestures downstairs.

'If you like,' she says, the welcome as gracious as it is linguistically clumsy.

Apparently we do like, since Mum is already halfway down the stairs. The interior is an underground cavern of whitewashed brick cooled by a fan. A skittle-shaped waiter circles lugubriously among the tables, taking orders and plonking non-matching plates of plain food in front of diners.

I'm halfway through my meal before I notice that every other table – apart from one near the kitchen, where the boss is playing cards with the woman we saw on the door – is occupied by an almost identical couple. On one side is a businessman in a flash suit with a briefcase by his chair and on the other a slender sybarite, barely out of his teens, in expensive track pants and trainers and sprouting jewellery from lips, ears, tongue and eyebrow. It looks like a scene from a digitally edited rock video, or a dream sequence in an expressionist German film. Deep below ground, out of sight of passers-by, this place makes an ideal rendezvous.

I wonder what the mother – or indeed this whole family, orthodox and Orthodox – makes of their clientele. Most likely they take the view any sensible restaurateur would take in a crowded market: regulars are regulars and you are grateful for them. And if a middle-aged tourist and his elderly mother take offence at (or even notice) the company they are keeping, the door is at the top of the stairs.

It's the end of day four, our last in London. The next week, the meat of the journey lies to the south-west. Mum seems happy that we've covered some of the city's essentials and, perhaps surprisingly, not even slightly fazed that we never saw Buckingham Palace, which she's 'seen often enough on the telly'.

What's coming up you'll never see on a television screen. It just wouldn't rate. If they did show it, they'd have to put it on after prime time when easily-frightened children are safe in bed.

WARM SOUTH

Mum doesn't need much persuasion to take a taxi to Paddington Station, which serves the south-west. We have left most of our luggage with the maid, a helpful Russian émigré called Inesa, who has wedged it carefully into tiny spaces in the concierge's cluttered office. But even though we have only a couple of small hand-held bags each, I manage to convince my parsimonious travelling companion that the hassle of locating and riding a couple of buses is not worth the small saving that may be made.

In the booming cavernous interior of the station, I stand and gawp at the overhead television monitors, which disclose the number of the departure platform only a few minutes before the train pulls out. No doubt this is a system designed to give the operators the flexibility they need to maximise the use of platform space. It certainly has the effect of focusing the minds of departing travellers. When the platform number winks up we have less than 10 minutes to make it to the train, which is plenty for an able-bodied traveller but is cutting it a bit fine when you have an orthopaedically challenged octogenarian in tow.

We are equipped with a couple of first-class Britrail passes, which, as I will soon find, entitle us to the luxury of a seat. The standard-class carriages are only marginally less comfortable than first class, but are often so overbooked that many passengers are left standing or squatting on their luggage in the entrance vestibules. In first class, by contrast, it's almost empty. We are given a copy each of the *Telegraph* (affectionately known as the 'Torygraph' by the readers of the *Guardian*, whom *Telegraph* readers deride as wet-eared, namby-pamby liberals) and plied with tasteless tea and dusty lukewarm coffee. The attendants also offer us biscuits but seem to have settled on an order of service which prescribes that the drinks and biscuits should be served about 20 minutes apart. After a while I get wise to this and grab a fistful of biscuits, which I reserve until the tea arrives. This apparently upsets the staff, who don't come back.

When we remark that we would like a cuppa, a pudgy, scowling attendant, whose name badge announces she's called Angela but who is less than angelic, rolls her eyes heavenwards and waddles off up the aisle. Half an hour later, as the train is slowing down to stop at Exeter, she arrives bearing freshly brewed pots of tea and coffee. We're standing by this time, assembling our bags and when we tell Angela we don't need it any more she looks highly affronted.

'But I've made it fresh for you!' she says in an injured tone.

'That's very kind of you, Angela, but …'

She looks suspiciously at me, perhaps wondering how I know her name – her own view of her name badge is apparently obscured by the last three of her chins – and explodes 'Never mind!' before stumping back up the aisle clicking her tongue and wondering at the stupidity of passengers in general and colonials in particular.

The English are fond of complaining about how unreliable their trains are, but their constant discontent is nothing that a dose of TranzRail wouldn't fix. The privatisation of track management has been a disaster, as the well-publicised crashes (along with Ken Loach's bleakly funny film *The Navigators*) show. However, the service itself manages a remarkable efficiency, and each company statistically quantifies the extent to which it has failed in graphs and charts at major stations, even undertaking to compensate regular travellers with free tickets when its performance falls below a given benchmark. It may be a cynical marketing ploy; sceptical locals I spoke to suggested that the benchmark was a standard of service that could be achieved even if half the staff were asleep and half the remainder were at the pub at any given time (in fact, some darkly hinted that this was the standard work practice). But in my experience trains left and arrived on time. In any case, on all but the most insignificant branch lines, if you miss your train, or it arrives late or not at all, it scarcely matters. Another will be leaving – or failing to do so – within a very few minutes.

It plainly impresses Mum. As we speed across Somerset she

looks out the window at the countryside flying past and concludes that, 'I think we'll make it before 12.30, by Jove.' How she can possibly hope to know this when she's travelling the route for the first time, God alone knows, but I decide against troubling her for an explanation.

At Exeter, we pile out and take a taxi to pick up a rental car. The hire process is a flurry of paperwork and decision-making, but soon we are looking over a near-new blue Ford Focus, which looks like a Dinky toy, and agreeing with the attendant as to the location and seriousness of some surface scratches. When we finally pull out of the hire firm's driveway into the light traffic of the surrounding industrial area, it has started to drizzle. I flick the windscreen wipers on. Nothing happens. I realise that the levers for the windscreen wipers and the indicators have swapped sides of the steering column since we changed hemispheres. I spend the rest of the day internalising this information. In the meantime I execute a handful of wrong turnings and corrective circumnavigation of traffic islands at major junctions with the wipers thrashing furiously while I leave other drivers to guess at my intentions. This they seem to manage rather well.

Fortunately the foot pedals haven't shifted, and I drive down progressively narrower roads towards the seafront at Sidmouth. This is what they call the Cornish Riviera, and the roadside signs proclaiming that fact tell you plenty about the locals' beach culture. The word 'riviera', coined to describe the stretch of coast between Cannes in France and La Spezia in Italy, sounds comical when applied to these fields and thickly wooded hillsides that roll down to the red cliffs and the icy sea west of Lyme Regis. It is a word that might conjure up visions of palm trees and casinos and cocktails by the pool, but the locals have the words emblazoned on a background of the ultimate symbol of the English summer – a bumper-sized ice cream.

When we hit the promenade at Sidmouth, the holidaymakers' behaviour in their natural habitat proves the accuracy of the image – as well as justifying all the old clichés about the way Poms behave on the extreme edges of their island. Along the seafront promenade, where the window boxes of houses and hotels brim with pansies, the sallow sunseekers stroll, covered from toe to neck, mostly topped with sunhats, and licking jumbo selections from the 99-flavour ice-cream parlour. On the beach, others sit in straight lines – never in conversation-friendly groups – on deckchairs (rented for 40p an hour or £1.40 per day) staring glumly out to sea. Perhaps they dream of the Caribbean. The glassy water is unbroken by so much as a single swimmer.

Here, near the end of the island, I am struck by the alienness of the place I have come to. The shore slopes steeply into the water and the tides, we are told, rise and fall more than 12 metres. The strangeness is embedded in the geography: the southernmost point is the country's warmest, the moon is upside down. But it is embedded in the language as well. What we call the beach, the people here call the seaside. It's a subtle difference of emphasis, but within it may be detected the different role the space between the land and sea plays in each country. To the English, the shore is a boundary – the side of the sea, no less – where the place man was made to walk becomes the place where he struggles to stay afloat; down under, by contrast, it is a playground, a stretch of sand where we may soak ourselves in the harsh sunlight we sought when we migrated south, always south.

Here, more than 50 degrees north of the equator, about as far north as the Auckland Islands are south, the locals are careful to cover up against a sun that has all the burning power of a 40-watt light bulb. The kids, who content themselves by rolling large toy trucks across the piles of pebbles (there are no sandcastles because there is no sand), wear hats and T-shirts. The adults are in shoes and socks.

There were no shoes and socks at Ngarimu Bay, only plastic sandals and they lay most of the time in untidy piles on the front lawn as we tip-toed, barefoot, wincing at the heat of the sunburnt tarmac, across the coast road to the beach.

The bach at the bay a few miles up the coast from Thames was a converted garage – its front door was a long, segmented affair that rattled around a curved track to hang all day along the building's inside wall. Within, curtains divided the space into makeshift rooms and a small kitchen filled an alcove. The simple surroundings were fine by us kids, who spent no time inside unless driven there by the weather, when we would read as the rain lashed the unlined tin roof or play endless games of cards or scrabble.

No pretty window boxes brimmed with well-tended pansies here. The garden was a desert landscape, its sandy soil planted with leggy geraniums. They snaked across the yellow grass, which crinkled dryly underfoot as we scampered for the beach; there we would roll in the waves for hours or build sandcastles on a grand scale. Heedless of the damage the sun was doing to our creamy and freckled Celtic skin, uncontrolled by parents who didn't know what skin cancer was, and apparently incapable of learning for ourselves from painful experience, we would slowly but fiercely grill our bodies beyond medium rare.

At night my burnt skin would turn cherry red, sometimes driving me delirious – on one occasion Dad actually injected me with a sedative drug to still my febrile night-time screaming. I would spend the next day glowing hotly in the shade, waiting just long enough to allow my burnt skin to moult in papery sheets before running out to present new, tender epidermis to the sun's unforgiving rays.

On other summers, we made the long drive from Hamilton to the East Coast, which seemed then, as it does still, like another country. In the family's ponderous and loyal turquoise Vanguard, we would grumble in low gears through the January dust beyond Opotoki, passing Maori kids, three- or even four-up on 16-hand horses, waving in enthusiastic greeting. The winding road would suddenly drop to small beaches where old men chatted as they mended nets on the pebbled foreshores, or river flats where women bent among rows of corn or kumara. The lush gardens, full of high corn so green it was almost blue, were constant reminders that we had crossed an invisible frontier into a world of sparkling unfamiliarity.

We stayed at Waihau Bay in a guesthouse that time has overtaken; it could not compete with the comforts of modern motels and these days the establishment is a backpackers' lodge. But then, Maori women woke us at 8 with their wooden trolleys rattling along the corridors of red-painted concrete, delivering a cup of tea to each bedside – no matter the age or appetite of its occupant. (My parents groaned at the intrusion but it was so embedded in the culture of the place it never seemed to occur to them that they could ask to sleep in.)

The women who cooked the massive meals had forearms like hams. Heavy china plates were laden with mussel or paua fritters, thick fillets of fish, gamey slabs of wild pork. Afterwards there were piles of cholesterol-laden desserts, curiously called 'sweets'. There was no menu – you ate what was served – but you went back for more until you couldn't.

The wharf, protruding above the pebble-strewn beach, was only a few paces away, the fish flashing silver in the green shallows for hopeful young fishers.

We head west along the coast, past a grand hotel with a croquet lawn out front, over the hill and down to the farmstay where we have booked for a couple of nights. The proprietor is a cheerful soul, so horsey that she just throws an apron over her jodhpurs and swaps her riding boots for fluffy slippers when she moves from farm work to domestic duties.

Her voice might have inspired the one Prunella Scales adopted so Sibyl Fawlty might hoot down the telephone 'Oooo, I knoooooow!' except that she would have been a teenager when that character was born. It's a piercing cross between a whistle and a honk, which is deployed – she has the extraordinarily irritating habit of completing your sentences for you – in the middle of anything I utter. Thus conversation with her becomes a race in which, before a thought is half spoken, she joins in and it becomes a contest to see who will get to the end of it first. It is extremely unnerving finding out what you are going to say while you are still saying it.

The seventeenth-century farmhouse backs onto a cobbled yard. A pair of wagtail spaniels loudly warn of a new arrival by lumbering over and barking furiously, though only after the strangers have been there five minutes and virtually unloaded their luggage. The dogs spend the day chasing each other's shadows and trying to get into the car every time I open the door. Birds lace the air as they sweep from barn to barn. I have no idea what they are, though I am sure I would recognise the names from the books of my childhood: swallows, perhaps, or robins. But they dart and swoop and shoot like bullets across the yard and there would be no danger of my identifying any.

In one of the stables, a farrier in a battered leather apron shoes the horses with work-stained hands using technology which, apart from the fact that the portable furnace on the back of his ute is gas-fired, has probably scarcely changed since the Middle Ages. He sits on a gnarled handmade stool, polished by his trousers to a golden sheen.

Mum feels more at home on a farm than I do. For a start, she likes horses, creatures I have always feared and loathed except when they are on distant hillsides or in western movies. I maintain a safe distance while Mum mooches around the stables patting and talking to animals that, if I came anywhere near them, would at least fetch me a heart-stopping kick in the sternum or more likely stomp me into a bloody paste that would have to be hosed off the cobbles. Horses are like that: malevolent and dangerous.

In the woman who talks softly to these long-lashed animals I can glimpse the girl Mum once was, at home on the farm in Drury. She used to speak often of those days, when she was an able rider at home in the country. But all that was left behind when she came to town and married a doctor.

I grew up seeing the countryside as a strange and hostile place. On holiday visits to farms, I was scorned by rural kids for my clumsy ignorant ways. If I went to the milking shed, I always contrived to get shat on several times, so quickly learned to stay in the separator room and make myself useful by taking a billy of fresh milk, warm and sweet and creamy, up to the farmhouse.

This unfamiliarity with the outdoors always seemed to me a betrayal of my birthright. At the age of six or so, I spent a summer week at a schoolmate's bach at Waihi. His elder brother turned up one day, having been fishing at Taupo, boasting of his catches. I listened, awestruck and dying to make a contribution to the big boys' talk.

'What kind of fish were they?' I asked, then, foolishly, added, 'Kahawai?' because it was the only fish whose name I could remember offhand. The room erupted in hoots of derision and I fled to the beach, my cheeks burning from shame.

I spent my ninth birthday on the Waikato farm of some of Dad's patients while my brother, who shares a birthday with me, was busy being born. I quickly learned to stay clear of the eldest and ablest of the family's daughters, who was contemptuous of my inability even to shoot the side of a barn with her air rifle; she could pick off small tin cans sitting on fence posts so far away I could hardly see them. I spent the day of my birthday alone on the camp stretcher they had set up for me in the corner of the lounge, deep in the pages of the Biggles book my parents had bought for me.

We head back into Sidmouth to eat, in the dining room of the Bedford Hotel, largely because it's the first place we see as we leave the car park. The staff seem to be all Australian or South African and the waiter who is serving us is being watched over by a pimple-faced youth who interferes at every possible opportunity, dropping and knocking things over each time. His apprentice nods solemnly after every demonstration, apparently convinced that this is the way to do it. I wait for him to pour a glass of red wine into my lap to prove that he should be placed on the permanent staff, but he appears to decide that he should wait for his mentor to demonstrate the correct way to pour a glass of wine into a diner's lap.

The à la carte menu looks a trifle dodgy, not least because everything that is plural (chops, scallops, potatoes) is garnished with an apostrophe and I make it a rule never to eat anything that is spelt wrongly. The schnitzel is not Wiener but Weiner, just as it is at home, but the local specialities seem to be haddock and plaice so we settle for the fish and chips, which arrive with a pile of peas into which has been dropped an extremely large teaspoonful of butter. I mouth a silent apology to the cardiologist and tuck in. Outside on the promenade, strollers are still hard at it. Mum natters and dawdles over her meal and I catch myself snapping at her to 'Eat your peas.' It is a chilling moment, not least because she seems to find it unremarkable.

Back in the room, I flick idly through the television channels as Mum fills out her diary, whispering to herself slowly as she writes. She records the quotidian details of the day's events, the meals eaten, the sights glimpsed. It's her way of remembering. On the table by her chair at home, where she sits and watches television, she keeps a small jotter and notes down the news she must impart and the questions she must ask when someone next calls. But it's also her way of stopping the experience slipping away. The sight is ineffably sad. Not for the first time, I seethe inside at the thought that she had to wait so long for this that it became an ordeal for a frail, elderly woman rather than an enjoyable undertaking for someone in the prime of early middle age, a joyous pilgrimage undertaken alongside the man with whom she had chosen to spend her life.

The farmstays and B&Bs in the English countryside take breakfast seriously. The proprietor stands before us in the dining room on equestrian legs, their bowed shape comically exaggerated by the protruding flaps of her jodhpurs. She recites the list of what she can cook, and I take the lot; but when it arrives it's plain it has never touched the inside of a frypan. Everything is microwaved into limp characterless blandness, a sort of breakfast stew. I nibble politely at it before we beat a retreat and head for the car.

At the nauseatingly pretty fishing village of Beer, the whitewashed houses open straight onto the winding streets, and petunias chatter gaily in the window boxes. The road drops sharply to the beach – a small bite out of a long line of red clay cliffs to east and west – where a long, thick rubber mat forms a path to the water's edge over ankle-twisting pebbles as big as cricket balls. A few holidaymakers are parked on the stones, fully dressed and gazing glumly at the icy water. Varnished clinker boats with inboards are available for hire but no one seems inclined to hire them.

Mum seems out of place here. She stares about her, as if willing something to happen that will justify the effort of the walk down. She strikes up a conversation with a couple from Yorkshire who come 'all this way every summer because we love it'. They are standing, a metre off the rubber mat, dressed as for a shopping trip.

Back up in the village I wander around looking for a strong espresso and end up in a shop whose sign announces it is a 'coffee bar'. There is nobody behind the counter and the almost-empty glass jug quietly festering on the hot plate of a drip filter machine is a deeply depressing sight. A woman emerges from the back singing at the top of her lungs.

'You're sounding very cheerful,' I observe.

'Always cheerful,' she bounces back, chewing the second word as though it has the letter 'r' three or four times in succession. 'No point in being miserable, is there?'

I begin feeling pretty miserable about my prospects of getting a cup of decent coffee.

'Coffee?' I offer hopefully.

'Coffee, yes,' she replies reaching for the heatproof glass jug.

'You don't have espresso, by any chance?' I wonder with no great hope.

'Do you mean …' she says, attempting a gurgling, spluttering, hissing imitation of a large espresso machine, 'with the frothy milk?'

'Yes!' I answer, with a surge of excitement.

'Not 'ere,' she says sadly. 'Oi don't think you'll find that in Beer.' She checks with her offsider out the back and returns to confirm it. If anything she's sounding more cheerful, delighted to have been able to oblige by confirming that I was correct. She sounds so proud that I feel I ought to look pleased.

We take the locals' advice not to drive into Exeter but instead to park on the outskirts and take a minibus into the centre. This sounds like an excellent idea but it proves a lot simpler to recommend than to accomplish. Driving around anonymous light industrial areas, I end up in a car park plainly labelled as 'park and ride'. But the security guard who takes an instant interest in our arrival informs us that it is reserved for the staff of a specific business. When I ask her where the park and ride is that anyone can use, her reply is classically British.

One of the things the traveller in Britain has to get used to

– at least outside London, where most people say things like 'Sorry, mate, I'm from Boise, Idaho and I'm looking for the can' – is the locals' predilection for offering directions that can only be understood by people who have lived there for years. Everyone's very helpful and willing, but equally all tend to offer directions of headspinning complexity, larded with references to local social history and dark goings-on.

'Go up the hill where the fire was,' one will say, 'not the one at Archie's place – poor Archie, he never really got over that, and then his wife left and, I don't know what – but the upholsterer's. Take a right down where Mavis used to 'ave the tea shop and you'll see it on the right. Are you from Australia?'

The other impenetrable aspect of the way these people give directions – in London and beyond – is the insistence on measuring distance in time. If you're driving long distances, this can be helpful. A two-hour drive is a two-hour drive whatever you're driving (well, almost anything, and if you're in an Austin A30 with worn piston rings or a strange make of car in which you cannot find any gear higher than second, you're likely to make your own adjustments). But when you're seeking to navigate city streets on foot, it becomes more problematic.

London's ancient streets curl and swoop and split off at odd angles, which makes it pretty meaningless to say something is four blocks away as the residents of the reliably grid-patterned New York can do. But what's wrong with using metres, or yards if you are, as the Poms are, doggedly clinging to imperial measurements?

What they say instead is that something is a given number of minutes' walk away. Now given the difference between my mother's hobbling gait and my brisk stride, measuring distance by the number of minutes it might take to walk it is about as helpful as suggesting that it's as distant as a piece of string is long. But the locals make up for this by simply inventing a number. Thus 10 minutes' walk can turn out to be five doors down the street or a long slog that would have been better undertaken by two changes of bus.

'… and you're there,' the security guard is saying. I drive off in the direction that her uniformed arm was last seen pointing.

A quarter of an hour later, I find myself passing her again, standing at the entrance of her park and ride. She catches sight of me and for an instant our eyes lock.

'*That* way!' she bellows, virtually hurling a white-shirted arm in the opposite direction from the one I'm driving. I return her wave as casually as I can manage, with a gesture that is meant to say, 'I *know* it's that way, you silly cow! I'm just heading down here to pick up a pint of milk.' I'm not entirely sure that it works.

After an indeterminate period of driving in concentric circles, each one usually, though not always, smaller than the circle before it, I finally glimpse a sea of parked cars and a bus shelter. It is on the other side of a four-lane arterial road. It seems as remote as Paris.

Eventually we find it and wait patiently at the bus stop as the heat gathers. The fare of £3.60 each delivers us into a city where parking looks about as problematic as in Te Awamutu on a winter Sunday.

I leave Mum on a streetside bench while I pick up a couple of leaflets from the tourist office. I emerge to see her across the street, deep in conversation with a heavily tattooed man with a voluminous beard, a shaven head and a stupid-looking bull terrier at his feet. He sits between two shopping bags crammed with blankets and talks in the slurping mumble of the heavily medicated.

I join them with a friendly nod but each time I try to bring their chat to a halt with an 'Oh, well, better get on, I suppose …' Mum launches off up a new conversational side road. Only when it looks like he's decided to offer us his services as a guide for the day does Mum accept the tug on my arm and we head for the cathedral.

We have a sandwich in the Cathedral Close in the shadow of the Royal Clarence Hotel, which, the plaque at its door boasts, is the country's oldest. It seems to me a pretty hard claim to sustain – a quick Internet search tells me that the Old Hall Hotel in Buxton, Derbyshire and the Old Bell in Malmesbury, Wiltshire make the same claim, cautiously qualifying it with the word 'reputed'. Age, of course, is what England sells itself with, particularly to Americans who have always felt a stinging sense of inferiority about coming from a country with only 200 years of history. But I find myself wondering how one can say when a hotel was born. A roadside tavern that allows a weary traveller to doss down in the barn in return for a few coins might be called a hotel but that was happening long before they set up Best Western.

I am sitting a few metres away from Mum, in the shade, and my back is turned as she wanders off to admire the trees, leaving her bag unattended. It's parked on a low wall, within easy reach of the passing foot traffic and Mum doesn't take too kindly to my little homily about keeping an eye on her belongings.

'Nobody's going to take it,' she scoffs.

'Oh, well, that's all right then,' I say. 'I'll contact the local constabulary and tell them to take the rest of the week off.'

The 117-metre-long cathedral has the longest continuous Gothic vaulted arch in the world, a fact announced alongside the notice that sternly suggests how large a visitor's 'donation' ought to be. This – the length of the arch rather than the size of the donation – would normally have bored me rigid, but the cathedral is so beautiful it takes the breath away. Unlike the Abbey, whose longevity it rivals, it is clean and uncluttered, although the schoolboy graffitists have got to work on the ancient tombs of a couple of bishops in the Lady Chapel. This impression of simple, elegant beauty is underlined by the coincidence that a visiting Italian choir stages a short recital of sacred music in the nave. Their pure voices echo silkily off the high ceiling and I remember what I liked about being in church.

I drive back along roads that are now becoming familiar – some, near Exeter, a good deal more familiar than I need them to be. We pass signs pointing to villages with quaint names like East Budleigh and Ottery St Mary (this last, it turns out, is the birthplace of Coleridge). We stop for a beer in a tiny and promising-looking pub in the promising-sounding Newton Popplewell. It looks attractive from the outside, but the bar is ruled by a pesky black labrador, which sniffs our crutches and our crisps while the barman – to whom the animal apparently belongs – smiles indulgently.

'Friendly, in't 'e?' he asks with a smile so broad it looks half-witted.

'Too friendly,' I reply, but he can't hear me over the whirr and beep of the poker machines, which fill half the small bar.

I find it hard to understand the tolerance that society has developed for dogs. If they were invented now – animals who dropped turds full of disease wherever they like, ran around smelling or even eating turds of others of their kind, infesting furniture and carpets with biting insects and regularly but unpredictably savaging little children and pensioners – they'd be immediately banned.

If children – or even adults – did any one of those things, they'd be locked up and they'd have a lot of trouble getting a court date. But we do more than tolerate dogs. They are regarded as charming and sweet, and people (like me) who object to being terrorised by slow-witted, territorially sensitive quadrupeds with slavering jaws full of teeth that can separate a man from his genitalia in an instant are seen as incurable curmudgeons.

Worse, those who do not classify themselves as dog-lovers are blamed for the behaviour of the dogs who act in extremely unloveable ways. 'It's because you're scared,' their owners say gaily as their animals stand, emitting a low growl, with their muzzle only a few centimetres from a tender part of your anatomy. They will add with evident pride that 'She senses it,' plainly waiting for you to applaud the dog's powers of perception.

'I've never seen him do that before,' is another favourite excuse, which is actually a thinly disguised suggestion that it was your own fault you got mauled.

'Rover's very intelligent,' they say hotly and get even more cross when I say that I suppose he is, compared to the fridge (though not, I suspect, a microwave oven of recent manufacture) and that, in any case, we only say he's smart when he does something we would have never expected him to do because he's so stupid.

Unlike some of the more radical fringes of the population

of dog-loathers, I do not advocate their extermination. Dogs are terrific for things like felling thugs armed with knives, sniffing out bananas in luggage, and finding people in collapsed buildings or avalanches. But man's best friend? I don't think so. My best friend has two legs, makes decent conversation and is happy to pick up the bill when we go out to dinner.

The barman wonders if we want another pint. I briefly consider asking whether he could whip me up a syringe full of dog tranquilliser but think better of it. Dog-lovers have a much poorer sense of humour for things that humans do, in my experience, than they expect us to have for things their animals do.

Back in Sidmouth, we park the car and go strolling in the town looking for postcards. Mum, attempting a jaywalking manoeuvre that would see her imprisoned in many countries, steps off the kerb and walks along the roadside of a line of parked cars. What happens next is plain only to people on the other side of the street. From where I am standing, she simply vanishes, accompanied by the sound a couple of kilos of stewing steak make when dropped from a height onto a marble bench. I run around the front of the car and see that she has tripped over the protruding tyre of a Mercedes angle-parked with its wheel on full lock. She has dropped like a stone, face-first on the tarmac and, five seconds later, she is still lying there. For a moment I think she is motionless, but then I realise she is trembling. Her whole body is rocking and, as she is helped to her feet by the solicitous passers-by who have gathered, I realise she is laughing.

For the next 10 minutes, I deliver her a stern lecture on the purposes of a public footpath. But she can't stop laughing and, in the end, I grudgingly join her. The damage is minimal, the graze on her hand almost a mirror image of the one she sustained when her neighbour's dog dropped her a few days before we were due to leave. I take her home and pour a couple of G&Ts – a stiff one for her and a very stiff one for me.

Dartmoor spreads like a stain across the south central part of Devon between Plymouth and Torquay. I know something of what to expect from Conan Doyle's *The Hound of the Baskervilles*, which was inspired by tall tales the author heard in the area.

I was raised in the home of a Sherlock Holmes fan. My father read every word Conan Doyle wrote and could quote long passages by heart. His passion was fuelled by the fact that the author was his godfather, a position he had accepted when Gramps gatecrashed a reception during Conan Doyle's 1915 visit and dropped the request in his lap. Needless to say, the prodigiously moustachioed writer was never called on to exercise the duties that went with the position – he died when Dad was 15 and, so far as I am aware, forgot his young godson existed before the New Zealand coast sank below the horizon on his return journey.

But we were regaled with the story as we grew up. It was never explicitly stated but we could read between the lines well enough: the family, in previous generations at least, was a cut above. Not for us the rather drab predictability of having local godparents – the useful kind who might flip you half a crown on your birthday or take you to the pictures; Dad's godfather was famous and, most importantly, an Englishman. Never mind that he never heard from his famous guardian who probably never gave him another thought (we saw no letter, and it's entirely possible the story was one of those self-sustaining family fictions, a kind of private urban legend that soon assumed the status of fact).

Certainly Dad was always more faithful to Conan Doyle than vice versa. The omnibus editions of Sherlock Holmes , along with the thick historical novels like *The White Company*, were near at hand, at boy-browsing level in the bookshelf by his desk in the living room. They shared pride of place with his other great passion, C. S. Forester, whose stories involving a midshipman called Hornblower were equally favoured among his insomniac late-night reading.

I cannot, to be honest, remember a single book of New Zealand authorship in my entire childhood. The shelves in the lounge were full of Dickens and Thackeray in which the world was captured in pages of grey type. Colour was to be found in the Time-Life nature books, celebrating the wonders of a planet on which I didn't seem to belong. Certainly my country barely existed and was not worth naming: the nature book maps always showed New Zealand as an unlabelled boomerang-shaped squiggle down in the lower right corner where it might be smudged by the page-turner's thumbprints.

My favourite was Pope's translation of Homer's *Iliad*. This was not because I was a precocious classics scholar or an admirer of its poetic merit (I still haven't read it) but because it had a soft and slightly furry leather cover, which I loved stroking. It also had gold on the page edges, and I often wondered whether I could scrape it off and sell it and be unimaginably wealthy. I knew the book intimately before I read any of the words, whose dense rhyming couplets were comprehensible only in phrases. It was that book that I imagined Keats holding when I read *On First Looking into Chapman's Homer* 10 years later. I loved Keats – his consumptive gloom suited my teenage self-image as a doomed romantic – and particularly the poem in which he expresses his rapture at reading a new translation, by the Renaissance poet George Chapman, of the *Iliad* and the *Odyssey*. I still recall the lines by heart:

Then felt I like some watcher of the skies
When a new planet swims into his ken;
Or like stout Cortez when, with eagle eyes
He stared at the Pacific – and all his men
Looked at each other with a wild surmise
Silent, upon a peak in Darien.

The shelves were crammed with treasures of English and classical literature, the corner cabinet bulged with sheet music and 78 rpm recordings – including whole operas – of work by stern men whose small plaster busts sat on the mantelpiece or piano top.

Amid all this, New Zealand work was scarce. So when I discovered a single local record adorned with a picture of a Maori canoe, it caught my eye. The ringing cadences of *Landfall in Unknown Seas* fired my imagination like nothing before it. It was recited in the vigorous voice of its author (the late Allen

Curnow was in his thirties when the work, commissioned to mark the tercentenary of Tasman's landfall, was recorded in 1949) and set to music composed by Douglas Lilburn. It was full of extraordinarily adventurous imagery: 'Suddenly exhilaration went off like a gun' or 'Who reaches / A future down for us from the high shelf of spiritual daring?' And there was such casually clever use of language; that awkward period in which departing sailors and farewelling crowds on the dock stare across the widening gap was condensed into the tidy phrase, 'Time to go and to be gazed at going.' But better, it dripped with an uneasy sense of what it was to be a white New Zealander: 'But now there are no more islands to be found and the eye scans risky horizons of its own.'

All this while, of course, dozens of other writers and artists in this country – Frank Sargeson, Colin McCahon and Janet Frame – were inventing what it was to be a New Zealander. But their attempts went unnoticed in our house where the shelves were stacked with Rodgers and Hammerstein, Gilbert and Sullivan, Forester, and Conan Doyle.

Only now do I begin to appreciate the intent behind Denis Glover's *Home Thoughts*:

I do not dream of Sussex downs
or quaint old England's quaint old towns
I think of what may yet be seen
In Johnsonville or Geraldine.

Dartmoor still had surprises for me. At the Church of St Mary the Virgin in Holne, they are celebrating the annual flower festival and there are cups of tea and home-made butterfly cakes for anyone happy to drop £1 in the saucer by the teapot. We sit in the pews pretending to admire the rather tatty flower arrangements.

'New Zealand!' enthuses the woman at the door. 'I have a friend in New Zealand.'

'Really!' I reply. 'Where does she live?'

'Oh, God!' she explodes. 'I haven't any idea at all.'

The fussy women at the church are not my idea of

Dartmoor. I wanted to see Baskerville hounds materialising out of the mist with fragments of Shetland pony hanging from their slavering jaws. Instead, the landscape seems almost benign, and far from fearsome. But as we drive into the park, the temperature drops sharply and I can fancy that the atmosphere of menace is thickening. I park mother on a small tor and take a photo in which you can practically see Daphne du Maurier in one of those fluffy cartoon thought bubbles above her head. Before we reach Princeton the mists swirl in. It is a brilliantly fine day on the coast less than 40 miles away, but here, as the grim hulk of HM Prison looms out of the damp haze, it doesn't seem summery at all.

We stop for lunch just beyond Princeton at a small, white-washed pub called the Warren House Inn. Under roof beams that would require a man little taller than me to walk stooped, we eat duck and Guinness pâté, Stilton cheese and crisp fresh-baked bread, sitting by a fire which has burned continuously for 157 years.

This might seem like an affectation or a fiction concocted to charm tourists and day-trippers from all-electric homes. The barman says the fire even survived the careful dismantling of the pub in the late nineteenth century when it was carried stone by stone to the other side of the road because the land was falling away under it. The burning embers, he tells me, were carried across the road and laid carefully in the new grate to flare up and burn on.

I enjoy the idea of this even if I am slightly sceptical about the detail. Retailing history as their best-selling primary produce, the Poms are likely to get a little fuzzy about the facts, as I will find out in a couple of days when I stand at the Mayflower Steps in Plymouth. After all, when the pub was being moved the fire hadn't burned for a record, or even remarkable, length of time so it seems hard to understand why they would have taken such care not to let it go out. And as the work of the graffitists in Westminster Abbey and Exeter Cathedral attests, reverence for history is a modern invention. The further we go back in our affairs as human beings the less conscious we are of our immediate past, much less posterity. The fact that tourists until the mid-nineties could get their photos taken on the Coronation Chair almost defies belief.

Maybe the pub-movers were reverent of the fire's then-short history. Maybe they didn't have a match and decided to transport the fire so that they would have somewhere warm to sit when night fell. Either way, who would have blamed them – and who would have confessed – if the shovelful of embers had cooled while they enjoyed their lunchtime pint of best bitter?

The mist rolls in across the moors – the sentence I have read a hundred times loses its ring of cliché and becomes a statement of unvarnished fact as I peer out the leadlight windows. The chill air licks through the open door, and I am grateful for the fire as we eat. The bar is almost empty, but we share a long fire-side table with two taciturn elderly blokes in tweed jackets and cheesecutters. Only the electronic beep of the cash register disrupts the sense that we could be in any decade of the twentieth century.

But the twenty-first suddenly bursts in out of the grey fog. Two groups of trail-bikers erupt into the middle of the bar, chatting thirstily as they jostle each other in the queue for service. One lot is dressed in cyclists' stretch suits in high-visibility colours and the other in fancy dress – Cinderellas and Beefeaters in running shoes and cycle helmets. It's hard to tell which is the more outrageous – those Spandex suits are most popular with people over 40, who should never, on any account, be permitted to wear them – but the atmosphere instantly evaporates. It's time to go.

WHERE THE MAORIS LIVE

Suddenly the hearse was moving. Nobody had asked me. They don't, though. You hire someone to make arrangements and they make them. Then you let go.

My father was making his last journey, from the church where he had reigned for so long as organist and choirmaster, to the crematorium, which sat on the neatly clipped expanse of the cemetery on the Morrinsville road west of town.

Standing on the gravelled yard outside the church, picking up conversations with people not seen for 20 years, I failed to register the significance of what was happening. Dad was leaving. (My inattention would have a bleakly comic sequel when, some time later, I finally realised that we should get going, I had extracted my mother and brothers from the welter of well-wishing and got them into a car. We had arrived at the crematorium gates just as Dad's brother was driving out. His cheerfully puzzled greeting – 'What happened to you chaps?' – told us all we needed to know. It was a moment of low farce, and it was easy to imagine Dad chuckling at the thought.)

The big rear end of the customised black Cadillac dipped on its springs as it bounced into the well of the roadside gutter and pulled with a 6-litre whine into the traffic. Then it came, a high keening wail, which pierced the dry February air.

'Haere, haere, haere,' called the Maori woman in the black dress. 'Haere atu ra.'

Her grey hair was crimped in a crown of roughly woven karaka leaves and a small frond torn from the same tree shimmered in her hand, which, according to custom, trembled with formal precision.

The crowd fell silent, less from respect for the mourner than for the moment. The hair bristled on the back of my neck and I felt a creeping in the flesh over my temples. It was perfect and perfectly touching.

It was only then that I noticed that fully a quarter of those at Dad's funeral were Maori. Until that instant, when the hearse began to crunch across the fine-gravelled yard, they had remained almost invisible, standing in groups behind a line of trees beside the church. They stood wordlessly in the shadows, swapping smokes, and dabbed the tears from their cheeks as a mourning went on that was alien to them.

Meanwhile, matrons in their floral frocks sought to embrace me and remark how much I'd grown. When last I saw them, they had been shapely housewives at leisure, some transformed by my fevered adolescent imagination into objects of sexual fantasy. Now, thick-hipped, greying and liver-spotted, they seemed impossibly ancient and their faces underlined the mortality the funeral had just spelled out.

My face was locked in a bland smile as I dribbled the same answers to the same questions: 'Auckland' or 'I'm a journalist' or 'Just the one – a son. That's him over there, the baby in his mother's arms.'

The prominent citizens of our childhood shuffled in and out of view, grey and gape-mouthed, calling to us boys but mixing up our names and wondering why no one answered. The ones who were once lawyers and doctors and successful were now superannuitants wearing slightly dazed expressions and the ones who were geeks and losers at school were now lawyers and doctors and successful.

The vicar moved like a galleon under sail through a sea of people. From time to time, a small spout of laughter exploded as funeral guests' memories bumped against each other. Ripples spread as the source of the laugh rocked backwards on the heels of polished shoes and the crowd moved to accommodate the stir.

It all sounded faintly forced to me, an unconscious incantation that sought to chase away the fear of death which had been conjured up inside. All the while the Maori watched from the shadows, watched this strange funeral, so cheerful and offhand. But when the hearse began moving unacknowledged by everyone, the watching stopped and one of their number thrust herself forward for the karanga.

It seemed for an instant almost surrealistically weird that so many Maori would show up at my Dad's funeral. These were people I had learned never to see even though they were never far away. Separated at times by less than a town planner's block, we nevertheless lived and moved in different worlds. But seeing them there, I suddenly realised that Maori had been part – if not most – of his daily life since he set up a medical practice on their doorsteps where the need and the opportunity were greatest.

But it never seemed that way for me. The country I grew up in – or at least the narrow slice of it where I walked – was one where the indigenous minority was largely invisible. My gaze, fixed firmly to the north where my bloodline led, never seemed to alight on Maori. They lived at the fringes of my world, and my schooling – rich in stories of Englishmen and Greeks, Romans and Americans, but empty of Maori characters – ensured they stayed there.

The land between our home and Dad's consulting rooms in Hamilton filled up a few years after our arrival with an enclave of state housing, where most of the families were Maori. The streets that laced the area were lined with two-storey semi-detached units, which must have looked homely on a public service drawing board but, a few years of habitation later, looked down-at-heel and drab. Wheelless or doorless cars sulked on wooden blocks in front yards bald of grass, years before such an image became a cliché.

Looking back, I suppose that it was the benign New Zealand 1950s equivalent of Chicago's projects or London's Brixton. The neighbourhood was not a pocket of poverty in the literal sense that word has taken on since the economic 'reforms'. Indeed, Dad often grumbled that every house he visited had a television; we didn't, but the point was more than a little spurious. We could have afforded a set in the early sixties – not easily perhaps, but without punishing difficulty – but Dad would never hear of it. He knew even then what it has taken the rest of us almost half a century to realise – that it rots the brain.

So this was not a slum in anything like the sense that most people would understand the word – the fifties and sixties were decades of full employment. But they were the houses of people who might have been living in another country.

I would peer into these strange lives from the window of Dad's VW Beetle while he made house calls. He never said I could come in, and I never quite understood why. Instead I waited in the car, fossicking in the debris on the floor for little souvenirs like expensive-looking pens adorned with the logos of pharmaceutical companies.

Occasionally pint-sized inhabitants of the house, perhaps tiring of adult talk about the illness inside, would come out to sit on the steps or swing on the gate. They would see me, I would see them and through the thick, flat window glass of the VW we would stare at each other. The precise nature of the gulf between us neither of us understood, but it occurs to me now that it was widened – and perhaps only existed – because so many of us were engaged in an unspoken agreement to pretend it didn't exist.

There were peach trees behind the surgery – we always called Dad's rooms 'the surgery' even though he was a family GP and the most complicated surgical procedure undertaken behind those mesh curtains was the freeing of an ingrown toenail or the sizzling diathermy of a wart. The fruit trees were older than the building, an unlovely fibrolite and weatherboard box which had been sited near the road-edge so as to preserve most of what was once the orchard of the house next door.

Mum would harvest the Golden Queens each summer, piling the bumper harvest into cardboard boxes and taking them home for bottling. As she plucked the fat fruit from under the leafy canopy, I would explore the edges of the section.

The right-of-way seemed just to appear one day, a new white concrete path lined with a cat's-cradle of wire-mesh fence and stretching off into the quick-growing tangle of suburban jungle beyond. I stood staring curiously in white-gusseted sun-hat as the fizzy smell of rotting windfalls stung the air.

The path, I knew instinctively, led to a foreign country. Perhaps Mum explicitly forbade me to head along it – I have no memory of that – but somehow I knew not to and never did. It was a part of town I never ventured into, even though it was the logical straight-line route from home to surgery and would have halved the journey time between the two places. I never went there because it was 'where the Maoris lived'.

They ought not to have seemed so exotic. I had spent the first few years of my life in Mangakino, a project town on the banks of the river in the south Waikato where much, if not most, of the workforce was Maori. Jean Tuwhare, the former wife of the poet Hone, told me years later that Dad had delivered a couple of their kids when Hone was working as a boilermaker on the hydro scheme there.

Mum recalls the place the same way most of her generation recall the mid-century – as a sunlit paradise where the term 'race relations' had no meaning at all, much less a highly charged one.

'There was no racial division in the town,' she recalls. 'The Maoris called *each other* "Hori". There was no racism in those days.'

It's easy, but unfair, to make fun of those words, as one might laugh at the idea that there was no such thing as gravity before Newton invented it. But in a sense it's true. There was no racism because we all *agreed* there was no racism. That word 'we' rather begs the question, of course. The smiling, self-abasing forelock-tugging Maori, a cliché of my early life, was a figure based on people who actually existed. But most Pakeha – and certainly those in the house I grew up in – accepted the comforting cliché as universally representative.

As we settle into the twenty-first century, we are just beginning to face up to the nineteenth; and we now know that many of the assumptions that lent a lustre to life in New Zealand in those days were a comforting veneer, which has chipped and flaked in the decades since. We – and here the word means anyone who cares to listen – now know that Maori discontent about the Treaty dates back to a few months after it was signed.

It was a discontent that many Pakeha have always seemed hellbent on ignoring. When I was at university, the engineering students had an orientation tradition of performing a mock haka. It was a clumsy, graceless, embarrassing thing, which reduced a powerful dance into a piece of crude slapstick. The engineers, who prided themselves on and worked hard to sustain their reputation as the vulgar, beer-sodden clowns of the campus, laughed off repeated approaches from young, radical Maori who implored them to drop the practice.

For years they were ignored until one day a group of activists who called themselves Nga Tamatoa, which means 'the young warriors', gatecrashed a 'rehearsal' and expressed their point of view forcefully but non-verbally. The event has passed into university legend. The point was taken. The annual haka stopped.

The part of Mangakino we lived in was known as Nob's Hill. The nickname was bestowed with a cheerfully self-effacing respect by those who didn't live there (and knew their place) and accepted with an only slightly self-conscious giggle by those who did. Mum and Dad landed on the hilltop – really just a small undulation in the riverside land – to live in unaccustomed comfort. They'd had their first child when Dad had barely started his medical training, and by the time he was installed as a poorly paid house surgeon in Auckland he was a father of three. Now he had a healthy salary and a free house.

'He was looked up to, all right,' Mum recalls. 'He was the only doctor there for the first year. He delivered 300 babies in that time.'

She can measure her prosperity by the fact that she had home help in those days (from a Maori woman, of course), which enabled her to discharge the duties as occasional cocktail party hostess imposed on her by Dad's position at the top of the town's social tree.

Barely a toddler, I was unaware of all this, of course. But unconsciously I was being inducted into the world I would grow up in, a world that was white and high-achieving and where Maori were out of sight. The gulf that divided me from Maori was not one of ethnicity but of social class. I knew – because my mother had told me, even if not in so many words – that these were not 'our' people.

Hamilton in the 1950s was a white town, which kept its Maori tidily out of sight. The place names of the parts of town told the story: Fairfield, Dinsdale, Melville, Frankton, Hillcrest. The streets I grew up in had names that were often prosaic (I grew up in Tramway Road) but sometimes exuded a whiff of our Celtic forebears (my teenage years were spent in Arran Road). My mates were called Hunn, Sunich, Smythe, Gilmour. They were the sons of immigrants, or perhaps of immigrants' sons. Some were Dalmatians, but most came down from English or Celts.

Even the newer immigrants, strange and displaced as they were, had the familiar ease of whiteness about them. I took a shine to a young Scot called Campbell (he pronounced it to rhyme with 'rumble') who arrived in my Standard three class, precisely because he seemed to me so improbably white. His Glaswegian eyes, perhaps struggling to cope with the bright sun in the land his life had brought him to, watered a lot. It's entirely possible he had always just finished crying; it was darkly rumoured that his mother or father or both were dead. I always fancied the eyes were stinging from the soapy bath-water from which he had only recently emerged. How else, I asked myself, could anyone manage to have skin of such unfreckled alabaster whiteness?

Scrubbed clean though he was, Campbell still got about in clothes stained from thrashing around on the grass in playground scraps, which, because of his pugnacious nature, he got involved in a dozen times a week. I stuck close to Campbell. Walking – and, when appropriate, cowering – in his shadow, I was able to feel like a tough guy without the tiresome duty of having actually to be tough. I enjoyed and tried with no great success to imitate the cocky swagger with which he walked, hands in pockets and bouncing on his toes as if always ready for a fight. It was a body language he doubtless learned in the mean streets of Glasgow but it was spoiled by the slightly effeminate way he would pull his jersey down over his arse. He was most given to this gesture – it was really a sort of behavioural tic – when attempting to look threatening, which was rather counterproductive.

'Yew, Jammy,' he would hoot, bouncing on the balls of his feet and tugging at the pullover hem, 'cum ear and see thart.' Within seconds he was on the ground, a whirling dervish in a bear hug with his antagonist. His style of fighting consisted in grabbing parts of the other's body and squeezing, which was reasonably effective if he had laid hold of a testicle (perhaps we weren't old enough to have descended testicles) though less successful if he had his arms round a thigh or a shoe. Since he fought with his eyes shut all the time it hardly mattered. He invariably lost, and the affray would come to an end with Campbell bouncing off down the road on the balls of his scruffily shod feet, tugging at his jumper hem and vowing to return with a secret weapon called 'ma bag berother'. This appliance never put in an appearance, and by the next afternoon, Campbell would have changed the subject by changing his target.

'Yew,' you'd hear him hoot, 'aye, yew. Whut didya say tae me?'

Tramway, then, and Peachgrove, and streets with names like Heaphy and von Tempsky, which celebrated the successful suppression and ultimate civilisation of the savages. There were no Maori names. Even the river was 'the river' and not the Waikato as it was in rural Tainui.

Maori were not utterly invisible. The home of Wi Te Tau Huata, a Maori cleric, was at the end of a long driveway over the entrance of which was erected an ornately patterned arch. It looked striking, if not strikingly odd, a visual shock among the anonymous façades of the state houses either side of it.

But for the most part, Maori were people who appeared in stories Dad told over the dinner table of patients whose only reason for living seemed to be to exasperate him. Many, probably most, of them were Maori, and he presided over their welfare with the kind of benign paternalism that befitted his station. He wore a three-piece suit, and only the pocket watch was needed to complete the picture of the avuncular Edwardian physician; from time to time he even had muttonchop whiskers. Patients welcomed him as 'Doc' when he padded up the front paths on house calls; this was less a nickname than an honorific befitting his status, which bordered on the shamanic.

That being so, perhaps there was some logic in the unilateral decision by Dad's second wife to take his ashes for scattering on the local marae in Kawhia, where he spent the last few years of his life. Perhaps he had a road-to-Damascus experience with the local Maori in his twilight years, when I saw little of him. But it seems to me improbable that it was profound enough to shut out his first family from his funerary arrangements.

Whatever happened in those Kawhia years, my father's attitude to Maori was cheerfully contemptuous. With the exception of a handful of clergymen – Wi Huata among them – whose ascent to the higher levels of the ministry always seemed to be regarded as a miracle of God's making rather than a triumph of the individuals' own enterprise, no Maori appeared on my childhood radar screen. Rescued at 11 from the levelling perils of the state school system, I lived a childhood as white as any Englishman's of my generation. I rode to school (on an English-made Raleigh bicycle) in striped blazer and baggy cap. At morning break we played conkers – an utterly English game in which we tried to smash horse chestnuts attached to strings – in the yards of schools as English as might be imagined. These schools lay at the end of long driveways whose sweeps were marked by lines of oaks or elms or yew. Maori boys were scarce on the roll – though the children of patrician Maori could get an Anglican education at Te Aute or St Stephen's. I remember only one in my six years of private school education and he was widely regarded (and appreciated) as the class clown and school jester. Shamelessly mugging for amused onlookers, he was every inch the perfect dag, the funny Hori. We loved him.

The neighbourhood has changed now as the composition of the city has changed. The primary school, Fifth Avenue, is a kura kaupapa Maori, called Te Ara Rima (the Maori equivalent of Fifth Avenue) and the signboard announcing as much is handsomely decorated with Maori motifs. But mine were different days. This was a city set up and ruled by Pakeha. I had not a single Maori friend.

It never occurred to me how odd this state of affairs was. Looking back at primary school photos, I see some Maori faces: the Tooman boy, Tommy Searancke, Ngatai Huata. I knew where none of them lived, with the exception of the conspicuous Huatas; yet I could have walked blindfolded to almost every one of my Pakeha friends' homes.

The four women clamber on at Oxford Circus. They scatter to various vacant seats and conduct an energetic debate as to whether they're on the right route for the British Museum. Their rapid-fire tinkling Spanish lightens up the atmosphere on the bus, which is otherwise occupied mainly by unsmiling Londoners.

The woman sitting next to me, plainly the only one of the group with a rudimentary command of English, asks the conductor for four one-day travel cards, which allow the user to use any public transport in central London for little more than the cost of a couple of single fares.

'Not 'ere, love,' fires back the conductor, a West Indian with a pure Brixton accent. 'Yew gotta buy that at the chewb station.'

The passenger's face drops and, as she holds up four fingers and presents a handful of coins for the conductor to pick through, I begin to realise that her disappointment is not at missing out on the cheap fare but because she doesn't understand what he said. My suspicions are quickly confirmed.

'Qué dice?' asks one of her mates.

'No sé,' she replies with a shrug.

The exchange ('What did he say?' 'I don't know.') brings out the amateur interpreter in me. I always jump at the chance to practise the Spanish I learned during two years in Latin America in the 1970s and have tried to perfect at every opportunity since.

'De donde son?' I ask. 'Where are you from?' is the question I was most often asked while travelling. In this context, it's a non-intrusive way of signalling that it may not be advisable to make jokes about the baldness or chubbiness of the quietly sweating man sitting next to her. But it's also an offer of help.

She's from Mexico it turns out and she embraces my linguistic facility like a long-lost friend. We chat away, while her mates strain to hear and toss inquiries and explanations back and forth ('Who is he?'; 'He speaks Spanish.'; 'Where's he from?'; 'Dunno. Sounds Argentinian?'; 'Rosa! What did he say? Rosa!').

We reach the Tottenham Court Road tube (the more elderly two of the quartet will only clamber off after I have said 'Si' about 10 times and nodded so hard I have a headache). Peering through the haze of diesel fumes, I point to the corner of Great Russell Street, which leads down into Bloomsbury and to the museum, before explaining the routine with the travel cards. We exchange the usual pleasantries, she complimenting me on my command of Spanish, I extravagantly demurring and insisting that I speak it 'muy poco'. We laugh together and for a long moment, I enjoy the sense of that fragile connection that language can throw across a cultural divide. She comes from the land where the Spanish colonised the Aztecs and Mayans; I from a country, the last in the world to feel the tread of any settler's foot, where Cornish and Celts landed among Maori. We have almost nothing in common – but for a moment we are talking the same language.

Months later, at home, I am driving through rush-hour traffic as the daily Maori-language vignette, *Rourou* plays on the radio. The speaker is engaging in some sort of debate. It's not a solemn discussion of weighty matters on the marae but a celebrity affair, recorded professionally in a theatre and broadcast as a piece of showbiz. He's speaking at speed, with passion and comic energy, though not, apparently, from notes. The audience is in stitches. I recognise a few words but have no idea what he is saying.

It's odd to feel so estranged from a unique part of my country's national identity. The more I travel the more I notice the casually polyglot proficiency of the rest of the world. The fluent facility of the guide on a Gaudi tour I took in Barcelona, who made her explanations at machine-gun speed in half a dozen languages one after another, was, one supposes, predictable enough. Hers was, after all, a job for which only those with a proficiency for languages might be expected to apply, and anyway much of her patter could have been learned parrot-fashion. But less expected was the competence of Manuel – a *nom de guerre*, surely – the porter, pool attendant and barman at the small private resort I once stayed in in Vanuatu.

Manuel took something of a shine to us and insisted on taking his day off to escort us to some nearby waterfalls to which, as tourists, we might have gained access only by payment of a stiff entry fee – if at all. We walked along the bush track accompanied by his young nephew, who buzzed around and ahead like a fantail, occasionally disappearing with a light splash into a river pool and emerging to run alongside us again, dripping in his shorts and jandals. Manuel told me how he'd courted his bride against the opposition of her family, since they came from different villages on different islands.

I was aware of the implication of what he was saying since I'd read in the guidebook about the archipelago's fantastic linguistic diversity. Some 105 separate languages are spoken throughout Vanuatu – including the colonial French and English and the pragmatic vernacular pidgin Bislama. That's staggering enough, but it's more staggering still to reflect that the islands once known as the New Hebrides are linguistically impoverished when compared to Papua New Guinea, where they speak 860 languages or Indonesia (670) or Nigeria (427). Vanuatu is twelfth on that particular order of merit.

'So,' I asked Manuel, 'I suppose you had to learn her village language so you could ask for permission to marry her.'

'Of course,' he replied, looking at me as if I were a simpleton.

'That must have been hard,' I sympathised, thinking back to the long hours spent on the verandahs of Andean hotels, hammering my way through Hugo's *Spanish Verbs Simplified*. Manuel winced at the memory of the effort it had taken.

'Yes,' he said. 'It took me very long time. One whole week.'

I applied myself to Maori for a lot more than a week. I set myself to learning the language, not once but three times, each time battling through traffic at the end of a work day to go to a night class. The most recent attempt, in 1990, was part of a sesquicentenary promise I made to myself to be more of a citizen in my own country. Yet somehow the language never bit deep into my imagination. Despite having learned – to greater or lesser degrees of fluency – five other languages in my life, Maori never seems to have set the synapses firing.

Cynics would say that's easily explained: the language is a dead one, of no practical use to a citizen of the world. That judgement, politically motivated rather than intellectually inspired, is in any case plainly false. Swedish or Dutch or any of the many tribal languages of Vanuatu are in good heart despite being of no 'use' outside the territories where they were born – and certainly of no use to Pakeha New Zealanders (the telling fact is that, unlike most Pakeha, most speakers of those languages are fluent in at least a couple of others including my mother tongue).

It seems fatuous, anyway, to say that Maori is of no use to someone living in the only country in the world where it's an official language. Saying it's no 'use' to speak Maori in this country is like saying it's no 'use' having a swimming costume or a pair of good walking boots. You can survive here with neither but you will never begin to understand the place.

That comment is not made from a lofty perch of having mastered the language – far from it. In my last year of hard work at night class, I learned barely enough to be able to hammer out a serviceable mihi – a ceremonial greeting – for any occasion when journalistic duty brought me into a Maori context. The first journalist who saw the fruits of that labour – the term seems apt since my mihi are always pretty laboured – remarked that it was a 'useful political tool'. The assessment may have seemed cynical – it was never so calculating – but it was not entirely unfair. My little learning was not undertaken solely to improve my journalistic access to Maori. But somehow it never fired an abiding curiosity about the culture of the people who were here before the whites – and the Whites.

The world always seemed like something other than where I was. The local travel journalist who once wrote that his favourite place in New Zealand was the departure lounge at Auckland airport was doubtless seeking to style himself as a man of the world for whom living on these islands was something of a tiresome duty. It struck me at the time as an extraordinarily pretentious statement, at once cringing and self-aggrandising. But the writer was perhaps unconsciously distilling a kernel of truth about the way many Pakeha New Zealanders see themselves.

The statement: 'I'm a New Zealander,' especially when uttered in the same breath as 'We are all New Zealanders,' seems more often a statement of defiance than of identity. It's a pronouncement regularly used to blunt Maori claims to a special sovereignty in this land, but it's become a fraught and problematic statement in the nineties when the pattern of our demographic fabric has changed so much. It's a fair bet that 'We are all New Zealanders' has not often been uttered by a Kiwi of English or Celtic descent to someone with an Asian face.

In mid-2002 a woman who works in the Auckland suburb of Howick wrote plaintively to the *Herald* on this matter:

Today I waited in a queue at a Howick bank. There were five people ahead of me. Three were Asian, two were Indian, both the tellers were Asian and the manager sat in her office – an Asian. The sixth person in the queue was me – a third-generation [New Zealander] of English descent, with blue eyes and blonde hair. Nobody was speaking English and I just wanted to cry. Today I felt like an alien in my own country.

Predictably enough, the letters that poured in oozed sympathy for her. It seemed to occur to no one that we are all immigrants here and that Maori must have spent the last 200 years feeling increasingly like aliens in their own country.

At times – often even – I feel like an alien in this country. Perhaps it's why that couplet at the end of Allen Curnow's 1943 poem *The Skeleton of the Great Moa in the Canterbury Museum, Christchurch* has a visceral effect on me: 'Not I, some child, born in a marvellous year / Will learn the trick of standing upright here,' it runs, and I feel the prick of tears at the back of my eyes each time I read it.

This is not to say I do not feel like a New Zealander. I have known the prickling sense of the hair rising on the back of the neck as I heard the haka performed or *Pokarekare Ana* sung under foreign skies. I have felt my heart almost break at the glimpse of a vista on the Coromandel or the Volcanic Plateau or of virgin Westland bush in a way that nothing in Florence or Provence or Arizona will ever speak to me.

Yet it has been a New Zealandness hard won, mined from a seam of Englishness that still runs through my life – and perhaps the lives of many Pakeha. The historian Jamie Belich has written of the process, which he calls 'recolonisation', by which we settled for being the most far-flung tribe of Britain, with a relationship to London 'closer to that of Kent than that of Kenya'. And I have spent much of my life feeling like an Englishman stranded on the edge of the world as far as may be imagined from my natural home. That was the way my parents wanted it, probably because they knew of no other.

When I was about eight, I decided to plant a tree in our backyard. Dimly, I suppose, I fancied it as a living testament that I had passed that way. I planted it slightly surreptitiously knowing that planting things in the garden was adults' work. Ignorant of the principles of silviculture, I planted it hard up against the fibrolite wall of the shed, where it would have no room to grow. Dumber still, the tree I chose was an oak. I knew that acorns made trees. I wanted to plant more trees with single-syllable, Anglo-Saxon names: ash, elm, yew.

I'm in Torquay looking for Fawlty Towers. Of course, I won't find it because it isn't here. It never was.

A few years ago the British Film Institute magazine *Sight and Sound* asked its readers to name the best British television series of all time. The 12 episodes of a frantic farce set in a Torquay hotel cantered home ahead of high-brow, big-budget masterpieces like *Brideshead Revisited* or *The Forsyte Saga*.

That decision would come as no surprise to any Fawlty fan. The show, written by John Cleese and his wife Connie Booth, was a comic masterpiece which perfectly captured the arrogance and eccentricity of the English and the problematic relationship between meek men and domineering women.

But that alone is not enough to make it the greatest show of all time. It seems to me that long-suffering Fawlty is such a marvellous character because he achieves what only the greatest of clowns can manage – a tragic grandeur that is almost Shakespearean.

Nowhere is this more poignantly expressed than in the climax to episode seven, *Communication Problems*. For most of us this is memorable as the one in which a deaf guest complains about the view from her window. Basil pulls himself up to his not inconsiderable height before asking:

'What did you expect to see out of a Torquay hotel bedroom window? The Sydney Opera House perhaps? The Hanging Gardens of Babylon? Herds of wildebeest sweeping majestically . . .'

In this episode Basil wins some money on a horse and, as he manically dodges circumstances that seem set to rob him unfairly of his winnings, he finally looks like he is going to get away with it.

'Don't you see, Polly?' he hisses to the maid, and there is something of Falstaff or Lear in the utterance. 'For the first time in my life I'm ahead!'

Of course he isn't, which is rather the point. But it's a moment in which Basil touches our hearts – as the best comic characters must – rather than just our funny-bones.

While it was set in Torquay, even the few exteriors weren't filmed there. The shots that opened each episode (rechristening the establishment anew each time, more or less anagrammatically, so it became Flowery Twats or Farty Towels) were of the Wooburn Grange Country Club near Bourne End in Buckinghamshire, which, sadly, burnt down in the late 1980s.

But the show was based on a real Torquay hotelier whose behaviour appalled Cleese and Booth when they were staying there while he was filming for *Monty Python's Flying Circus*. Donald Sinclair, the proprietor of the Gleneagles Hotel in Asheldon Road was the inspiration for Basil, Cleese has often said.

Sinclair was a navy man who disembarked early from that career because his wife convinced him they would make more money in the hotel business. But his military training had plainly not equipped him for life in the hospitality trade. The stories the Python boys tell – the bar locked during daylight hours, a suitcase thrown out of a window because 'it looked like it might contain a bomb' and a hectoring interrogation of breakfasting guests when a teapot went missing – make it sound like the television version of Sinclair was, if anything, milder than the real one.

Sinclair died in 1981 aged 72, which presumably makes the Gleneagles Hotel safer now. His widow, Beatrice, now in her late eighties and living in Florida, has lashed out at Cleese for holding her husband up to ridicule, but a woman who worked a summer season at the Gleneagles in 1973 reckoned Fawlty was a fair likeness of his real-life model.

Unsurprisingly, perhaps, Torquay has tried to disown *Fawlty Towers*, presumably on the grounds that it doesn't do anything for its image as a modern tourist resort. The woman in the tourist office turns particularly frosty when I mention it. She is making circles on a map at the time, marking the must-see attractions for a man who has only a day to spend in town.

'And I don't suppose Fawlty Towers is still around?' I ask

disingenuously. It is a bit like poking a caged bear with a stick since I know the answer. But I want to see how she might deal with a tourist who doesn't seem to know the difference between fact and fiction.

'That's not here,' she says baldly, folding the map and thrusting it into my hand. She begins to take a close interest in what is written on her desk calendar, which, as far as I can see, is only a Gary Larson cartoon.

'Well, I know *it's* not here,' I say.

My inspiration is the scene in which Basil chuckles to a doctor diner who he imagines is something of an oenophile that most of the hotel's guests 'wouldn't know a Bordeaux from a claret'.

'A Bordeaux *is* a claret,' his guest replies dryly.

'Well,' splutters Basil, 'of course, a *Bordeaux* is a claret.'

I try to imitate the same cadence as I repeat 'I know *it's* not here …' but she seems to have lost interest in me.

We would have stayed longer in this jewel of Torbay if she had sent me on a wild-goose chase. The best she comes up with is a tourist castle and the 'medieval' thatched village of Cockington, a sickeningly cute precinct with neatly trimmed lawns and crushed-shell paths. The public toilet has a thatched roof, as medieval public toilets presumably did. But children squawking to be released from their strollers and adipose mouth-breathing tourists peering through video camera viewfinders rather disrupt the atmosphere. We barely leave the car.

It's not hard to understand Torquay's unwillingness to be associated with a psychopathic hotelier who insulted his guests. But it does seem a bit short-sighted. Tourists who think that a television comedy classic has some value as either documentary or consumer watchdog are probably about as common as those who think there really is a hotel in Torquay called Fawlty Towers. And it seems to me that if you want to attract visitors to a beach resort on the Cornish Riviera when the real Riviera is only a £29 flight away (and not a lot dearer than the pretend one), you should believe in the adage that there's no such thing as bad publicity.

Fiction, after all, was the business of Torquay's most famous resident, Agatha Christie, who was born here. There's a room dedicated to her at the city's small museum, full of theatre programmes and costumes used in television adaptations, which occupies an hour or so of our afternoon. I toy briefly with the idea of looking up the Gleneagles Hotel in Asheldon Road, but I figure the present-day proprietors might offer me a welcome even more frosty than that of the woman in the tourist office. In any case, I reason, they are scarcely to blame for the ineptitude of a previous owner. I leave them in peace and we drive on.

History is best consumed in easily digestible packages when you're travelling. Piles of books, each new one contradicting or at least slightly skewing the version of the last, just make for a headache. Facts are best served pre-chewed without the garnish of qualification.

Now that I look at the photograph tucked behind cellophane in the album, the plaque on the seafront at Plymouth doesn't actually say that we are standing on the spot. 'This tablet,' it says, 'commemorates the departure from Plymouth in May 1839 of the *Tory*, the pioneer ship in the colonisation of New Zealand.'

But it is more than suggestive. We are standing where history was made, it seems to say, where hopeful emigrants stepped, in a single movement, from the past into the future.

'So it was here,' Mum says, her voice tailing off and her gaze setting sail. In her mind's eye the barque *Westminster* is tied up alongside. Apprehensive men in their stained Sunday best and women in long skirts and petticoats cross creaking gangplanks. Henry and Priscilla White are among them, perhaps, the long and anxious trip from Penzance behind them but a much longer and more anxious one ahead. It is December, 1842.

I struggle to find a decent camera angle that takes in the 'Mayflower Steps' and crops out the small ferry tied up to them and the bellowing hawker offering ''arbour tours. See the Eddystone Rocks. Last chance. Leaving now.'

'Course it wasn't 'ere,' says a voice beside me. Its owner is a grizzled superannuitant, with knife-edge creases in his trousers and a pure-white pencil moustache. He is staring down towards the warren of streets they call the Barbican and clinking the change in his pocket, as if to underline his complete indifference to whether I am interested or not. I am.

'It wasn't?' I ask.

'Nah,' he scoffs. 'This is just for the tourists. The steps are over there.'

With this he prods a wrinkled finger and I swivel around to look where he's pointing. There, on the opposite side of the street, is the whitewashed and dark-battened façade of a pub called the Admiral Macbride.

'Let me get this straight,' I say, zipping my camera back into its bag. 'You mean …'

'In the ladies' loo, as a matter of fact.'

His view is backed up by the cheery barmaid in the Macbride. She says she'd be happy to let me go into the ladies as long as there aren't any ladies in there, but there's nothing to see. The steps are there, but they're buried. On top of the last place the founding settlers of America stood in England they built a lavatory where tipsy women could totter after one too many Bacardi Breezers.

It makes sense when you read between the lines of the brass plaques that are affixed to almost every vertical and horizontal surface in the neighbourhood of the 'Mayflower Steps'. Sutton Water, the inner harbour where Plymouth pleasure craft now bob gently, is 'much smaller' than when Drake's flagships were tied up here, one plaque says.

Island House, in which at least some of the Pilgrim Fathers spent their last night in the Old World, is now the tourist office. Once at the water's edge, it is now separated from the harbour-side by a narrow road and a wide promenade on which they've plonked a huge public toilet, although at least they covered only water and not a historical staircase in doing so.

The *Mayflower* pilgrims did in fact leave from here, but that was never their intention. The hopeful travellers only ended up here because of a couple of false starts.

They had left Delftshaven in the Netherlands in a ship called the *Speedwell*. The name turned out to be soaked in a rather bitter irony since they had to put into Dartmouth, further east, leaking heavily.

From there she set sail again in August, 1620, only to return to Plymouth because they were still shipping water. Modern historians are agreed that this leakiness was less likely to have been caused by inherent structural weakness than by many small holes below the waterline, clandestinely drilled by the crew who were anxious to back out of what they thought was an unattractively dangerous contract.

In any case, the water slopping ominously round in the bilges was enough to dissuade about half the passengers from making the trip. They headed back to London and historical obscurity on the leaky *Speedwell*; the others, having secured a new vessel whose name has passed into legend, sailed on September 6 and wrote their names in history.

William Bradford, the voyage's very busy official scribe, remarked of those who stayed behind that their 'hart and courage' had gone. 'Those that went bak were for the most part such as were willing so to doe,' he wrote, 'either out of discontente or fear that they conceived of the ill success of the voyage, seeing so many croses befale & the year of time so far spente, but others in regard of their own weaknesse.'

Bradford can't resist a parting jab at the 'weaknesse' of those who decided to abandon ship, but from the vantage point of the twenty-first century, their anxiety is easy to understand. The *Mayflower* – and this was the good ship, remember – was just twice the length and barely three times the breadth of a double-decker bus, which has capacity for about 60 seated passengers. In this small space, almost 150 including crew were to live for a long sea voyage.

But if Bradford seems harsh, history as retailed in brass plaques at tourist spots is a little romantic. The Pilgrim Fathers – and there were mothers aplenty among them, as the passenger list shows – were the remnants of a group halved by seasickness and fear. That's the bit plaques and most history books don't tell you.

This romanticising of history, abetted by television's costume dramas, rather sanitises the reality. Historians will tell you that if time travel ever became technically feasible, it would be perilous for a citizen of the twenty-first century to travel much further back than the late nineteenth. I always fancied dropping in to

Shakespeare's London to see how the first performances of *Hamlet* or *King Lear* compared with the interpretations I grew up with. But those who know more than I do about those days are quick to remind me that I wouldn't see much because I'd spend most of my time doubled over and vomiting. The first thing we'd notice about the past is the bit no plaque or model or re-creation can convey: the nauseating stench of unwashed bodies and unhealed sores and rampant flatulence and rotting refuse pitched into the street or the rancid river.

The same smell would no doubt have hung over Plymouth as Henry and Priscilla took ship. But another smell would have been added to the olfactory melange, acrid above the heavy fug of daily life. Here, on the seafront, where one day a pub would build its ladies' loo, the air would be filled with the scent you find in the pens at the head of killing chains in freezing works: the sharp smell of sweat when it is laced with fear.

Plymouth, it turns out, is hiding another fiction – or at least retelling history in a way which shuffles inconvenient facts quietly out of sight. We clamber aboard an open-topped double-decker bus for a tour of the historic port city. It snakes up the hill and almost immediately passes the Hoe where, I was raised to believe, Sir Francis Drake was playing – and blithely continued to play – a game of bowls when news arrived that the invading Spanish Armada had appeared on the horizon.

The story had fired my imagination as a young boy. Not far from the furry copy of the *Iliad* in the family bookshelf was a selection of poems by Sir Henry Newbolt, which included a stirring piece called *Admirals All*. It was essentially a celebration of some of England's great sea captains, written in an affectedly martial style that made much of the stiff upper lip. Nelson's famous deliberate failure to see the signal to retreat at Trafalgar is rendered: 'He clapped the glass to his sightless eye / And "I'm damned if I see it" he said.' The refrain ran:

Admirals all, for England's sake
Honour be yours and fame
And honour, as long as waves shall break
To England's peerless name

Drake's offhand bravery made another verse:

He was playing at Plymouth a rubber of bowls
When the great Armada came;
But he said, 'They must wait their turn, good souls,'
And he stooped and finished the game.

Looking back it seems distinctly odd that such events – much less such pompous doggerel – should have so deeply impressed me. But the fact is that I arrive in Plymouth knowing much of the city's place in history. The historic departures from this port – the *Mayflower*, Drake, Nelson, Scott and Chichester – are all parts of stories that I don't need explained to me as the Americans and Italians and Germans do. They know their own history and regard the English one as foreign. But for most of my life I would be hard put to find a place in New Zealand where I could park the car and step immediately into a history I am familiar with.

The Hoe – essentially a wide expanse of grass on the hill-top – isn't looking particularly historical as we pass. The BBC children's programme *Blue Peter* is filming there and the place swarms with little holidaymakers mugging for the camera and trying to steal more than their allocation of the crew's give-aways of sweets and souvenirs. The kids' screams fill the air; but not enough to drown out the tour guide's commentary, which allows that the site of the game of bowls – if it took place at all – was almost certainly under the adjoining fortress.

But was Drake so unfazed by the arrival of the great seaborne enemy? Was he even playing bowls? The historians are sceptical to say the least.

Harry Kelsey in *Sir Francis Drake: The Queen's Pirate* (Yale University Press, 1998) says Drake and the other captains of the English fleet were only 'supposedly' playing bowls when word arrived that the Armada had been sighted.

'Rather than going immediately to his ship, Drake said that there was "sufficient time to finish the game and then finish the Spaniards too". His exact words vary from one telling to the next [elsewhere it is "... beat the Spaniards too"] primarily because no eyewitness account of the incident has ever been found.'

The earliest source is a pamphlet published in 1624, 36 years – the thick end of a contemporary lifetime – after the invasion. The pamphlet, written by Thomas Scott, an English clergyman, is, perhaps tellingly, entitled *Vox Populi* ('The Voice of the People'). It is, says Kelsey, 'a fictional account of discussions by Spanish noblemen, one of whom said that the Armada arrived off the shore "while their Commanders and Captaines were at bowls upon the hoe of Plimouth".'

That pamphlet, according to historian John Sugden in *Sir Francis Drake* (Henry Holt and Coy, NY, 1990) quoted a Spanish boast that the Armada approached 'so cuningly and secretly that the commanders were at bowls upon the Hoe and that the Spanish admiral might have surprised them at anchor'.

A century passed before Drake's name was even connected with the game of bowls (in William Oldys' 1736 *Life of Raleigh*) and the direct quotation is later still. In any case, some sceptics have observed that bowling on public ground was forbidden at the time – although presumably if you're about to save your country from an invasion by a fleet of Catholics, the authorities aren't going to pester you over the niceties of civic regulations.

The point remains that one of the most enduring stories in British history, which has Drake's unflappable calm restoring equanimity among the observers, is based on no credible authority. What documentary evidence exists is reportage many years after the event and, in any case, it seems to be a Spanish boast of naval cunning that does little for Drake's reputation.

What is more, records of the British response to the Armada's arrival make it clear that the onshore winds favoured the Spanish advance and not Drake's immediate response. In other words, Drake had no need to hurry, since he knew he had to wait for a wind change before he could make any serious progress. As it was each ship had to send out a small boat ahead, which would anchor and draw the larger ship forward on a cable. They waited by Eddystone rocks and the wind changed overnight. The rest is history.

Drake's gesture of bravado – and reminders of his victory –

were much rehearsed in wartime Britain when it was again under threat of invasion. Comforting fictions may be no bad thing in a time of war but the passage of years does not make them true.

The bus completes its circuit and drops us back at what I have already come to regard as the 'Mayflower Non-Steps'. Plymouth is a rather drab city whose centre was badly (well, actually, rather well) bombed in the war and rebuilt by civil service architects who would have felt at home in East Germany. We wander through the narrow streets of the area known as the Barbican and I fancy I can see the press gangs in the side lanes, mugging fit young men to haul them off into sea service.

At least they are not fudging the history at the Plymouth Gin distillery. It was built in 1425 as a Dominican friary and later became a debtor's prison. It is, the guide tells us, the oldest on its original site (it has been there since 1795) but only one wall, now part of an in-house café, remains of the original building.

I enjoy his demonstration of the distilling process and the chance to handle and smell the sweet herbs that infuse the pure spirit to make gin. There's juniper ('genever' in Dutch, which is where the drink gets its name) coriander, cardamom, angelica, orange and lemon zest. I inhale their heavenly scents and wonder why they smell so nice and gin tastes so vile.

Plymouth marks the end of Devon. Across its river, the Tamar, is Cornwall. Mum spends much of her time in Plymouth correcting the locals' pronunciation of it. Even the guide on the open-topped bus gets the benefit of the considered view that it is 'Tar-mar' and not 'Tay-mar' as they would have it, and my repeated flailing kicks at her shins quite fail to silence her.

'They don't know what they're talking about,' she scoffs as we negotiate the cobbled pavement and climb the steps into a tearoom.

Although we're not in Cornwall yet, there are Cornish pasties on the menu and we decide to try them. I'm a big fan of the 'When in Rome' rule, which doubtless explains why I ate exclusively German food when I was in Berlin, since there was perfectly edible food available from restaurants specialising in other ethnic cuisine.

The 'a' in pasty is universally pronounced as in 'plaster', not as in 'pants' and certainly not as in 'paste' and I am relieved that Mum does not start remonstrating with the young waitress about this. But when it arrives I rather wonder whether I ought to send her out to the kitchen to give them a bit of a rundown on the recipe.

She can speak with some authority on the subject, after all. The Cornish pasty (with the reliably antipodean 'a' as in 'pants') was something of a house speciality as we grew up. But it was a pasty few Cornishmen would recognise, for the simple reason that it tasted good.

To be fair, I should say that Plymouth is not in Cornwall but in far-west Devon. What's more, the oddity this tearoom served up as a Cornish pasty may not even have been the Plymouth standard. But it certainly isn't what I've been raised on.

This version is not the small, coffee-bean-shaped package with a crimped ridge of pastry on top, but a sideplate-size drum-shaped thing. It looks deliciously golden on top but the interior holds a bland, grey, crumbly mince and some roughly diced chunks of potato. The only apparent flavouring is white pepper, although laboratory analysis would probably detect traces of onion.

Only when I apply liberal quantities of Worcestershire sauce and the other locally popular condiment, brown sauce, which oozes messily from single-serve sachets, does it begin to acquire some semblance of taste.

The distinctive crimp was always part of the pasty's design, and for good, functional reason: it's a mark of the pasty's history as the world's oldest takeaway food – a portable and hygienic meal for the tin miners on whose broad backs Cornwall's wealth was built. Far below ground where there was no clean water, the miner held his lunchtime pasty by the rolled edge with hands contaminated by mine dust which often contained arsenic. Thus he could eat everything else, like cleaning off a corncob, and discarded the ridge uneaten.

There is plenty of debate about what constitutes a genuine pasty. Both short and puff pastry have their advocates. Some say the ingredients must be pre-mixed, others that they should be arranged in layers. Culinary historians have turned up recipes that prescribe a meat filling for two-thirds of the pasty's length and a jam filling for the rest – thus combining main course and dessert in one handy package. Fierce argument rages about whether the crimp should be on the top or the side, although the difference is rather academic once it's in position in the eater's hands. But the published research is unanimously of the view that ingredients must never be cooked before they are wrapped in the pastry. Each pasty must be baked completely from raw.

It's a point Mum is quick to make as she picks distastefully at hers. The filling, mainly cheap mince, may have been raw when it was placed in the case, but I suspect it had more flavour then. It's a little sobering to find that a fabled English dish was much better cooked in my childhood on the other side of the world. Certainly the New Zealand housewife of the 1950s had much better ingredients – particularly high-quality beef – available to her than the hard-pressed tin miners' wives, who developed the dish. The New Zealand version, packed with lean beef from cows which grazed on lush pasture and rolled in pastry shortened with the world's richest butter, simply didn't have the ingredients of the original.

That, presumably, is also why the meat-loving Argentines' small snack-sized version of the pasty, called an *empanada*, is so delicious. But the memory of the native Cornish pasty – I would not, despite a sampling regime that soon came to look more like foolhardiness than research, find a better one in Cornwall – still makes me shudder.

I take the subject up with a landlady of a pub near St Austell, deep in the heart of Cornwall, who promises that her pasties are the best in the county.

'Why do Cornish pasties taste like shit?' I ask, although I don't use precisely those words. From memory my exact phrasing is, 'The Cornish pasties I've tried have been not at all what I expected.'

'Oh?' she says, though it is something more like a snarl and I can see that she thinks I am some sort of smart-arsed whinging foreigner. 'What did you expect?'

I am about to say that I expected something that tasted edible, but at the last minute I think better of it.

'Well …,' I stammer, casting about for a diplomatic phrase.

'Most of them are rubbish,' she spits, prodigiously irrigating the front of my shirt. I can't help hoping that she isn't in the habit of enunciating this particular judgement while baking. 'They're all for the tourists. The only real pasty is home-made.'

She then launches into a detailed list of ingredients and the method of their preparation and assembly. Fortunately, Mum is on hand to correct her when she makes elementary errors of which, to judge by Mum's interruptions, there are several. She emphasises the quality of the ingredients and says that real pasties, made the right way, are delicious but expensive and that fierce high-street competition for the snacking tourists' discretionary spend has driven quality down.

I notice that her pasties are more expensive than most, so I look forward to tasting one. It tastes like shit.

We speed across the river whose pronunciation is uncontested – by me at least – and on into Cornwall. The rain, which has stayed away since we left Exeter, lashes the landscape now, falling in slanting sheets and making tidy silver ticks as it bounces off the tarmac. The wipers on the Ford slap and chatter. I retune the radio.

At St Austell I turn off the highway and steer the car through the narrow streets looking for a pub. We pass plenty; but in these parts the old, now revoked, licensing laws that required pubs to close their doors for a few hours in the afternoon have become embedded in local custom, and after several long minutes of navigating the snaking streets I fail to find the happy combination of an open hostelry and a legal parking place. I give up and point the car south towards Heligan.

Mum's lifelong passion for gardening has not been genetically transmitted. Her sons' teenage years were blighted by being pressed into service as poorly paid lawn-mowers. Gardens for us were collections of trees and shrubs that were alien to the landscape in which we lived. These exotics – no New Zealand natives cluttered our horizons – surrounded expanses of green sward, which did. For most of our young, lawnmowing lives we lived on a plot of land that was the complete Kiwi quarter-acre. This is an allotment whose size you don't really appreciate until you reach an age when you become responsible for regularly shaving it to within an inch of its life.

I secretly and deeply resented it when my turn came. But I could not completely deny responsibility for maintaining a lawn that was, for me, just a cricket ground surrounded by trees. A quarter-acre is a bastard to mow but a godsend to a cricket-mad kid. Our backyard accommodated a full-length cricket pitch on the diagonal between the feijoa and the hydrangea. The wicket was backed up by a tatty but adequate box net, which allowed a three- or even two-man match to proceed without the need for a wicketkeeper. It allowed only a short run-up, and when we billeted fast bowler David Larter during the 1961 MCC tour we thrilled to his long, swooping approach; it started at the compost heap and wound through the orchard until he burst from the foliage on his delivery stride.

The maintenance of this sort of backyard playground meant a heavy duty of mowing, a task which fell in turn to each of us when we reached the age when we could safely use the mower. It seemed to me that this piece of garden machinery was designed to perform one function: to fail to start. Most times, mowing the back lawn was a job that would comfortably fill a day, only an hour or so of which was spent with the mower actually running. The rest of the time was spent standing at a safe distance, while Dad, a hand-rolled cigarette drooping from his lips, sat on the grass performing emergency surgery on the decrepit Masport.

This surgery, were it being performed on a human, would have attracted the attention of half a dozen regulatory authorities for its breathtaking fecklessness and incompetence. The procedure was seldom actually dangerous to the mower, since

Dad, having no idea what he was doing, was unable to do much harm or any good. However the close association of a glowing cigarette end and a small reservoir of oil-enriched petrol posed a danger to the surgeon and his operating assistants. Dad would remove and clean the spark plug and saturate the sponge air filter with a small cupful of fuel, before tugging repeatedly and with steadily declining energy and conspicuous lack of success on the start cord. Nothing daunted, he would then set to attacking various screws and nuts, more or less at random, removing the engine cover or the top of the carburettor. Occasionally, if not usually, this process – interrupted for breaks in which he would slurp strong tea from cups smeared with his oily fingerprints – would end up with his piling an assortment of nuts, springs, cords, screws and mysteriously shaped parts into a cardboard box and loading it and the skeletal hulk of the Masport into the boot of his VW to drive it up to the repair shop.

There it would get prompt attention from the serviceman, one Mr Smythe, who was a patient of Dad's and didn't hold with the idea that the family doctor should wait his turn. This man, a sallow, slow-talking figure in an oily grey apron would haul the mower onto his workbench and quickly restore the contents of the cardboard box to the places where they belonged. All the while he concealed beneath a cheerful veneer the exasperation he must have felt. He must, at least once, have felt inclined to ask Dad how he would feel if one of his patients – a lawnmower repairman perhaps – turned up, bleeding, at the surgery having attempted an appendectomy or the excision of an ingrown toenail at home and said, 'Jeez, Doc, I seem to have made a bit of a mess of this. Can you sort it out for me?'

When I was about 12, Mr Smythe exchanged his grey apron for a starched white one and took over the greengrocery next door. I can't say for sure that it was Dad's regular visits that drove him to a mid-life change of career, but there was definitely an insouciant sparkle in his eye and a spring in his step as he swung himself whistling into his delivery van, his hair impeccably Brylcreemed, a pencil tucked behind his ear.

Mum is looking forward to Heligan, the 'lost gardens', which have become the most visited in Britain and now attract 400,000 to tread the paths each year.

We arrive at the gates as the sun sets and the air begins to cool and follow the signs to our lodgings. We pull up on the crunchy pebbled driveway of the Wagon House, in the garden's outskirts. The building has been immaculately restored to make a home and attached guest rooms but the high, wide, semi-circular front windows speak of its past life, as the building where the wagons were kept.

Spaniels – which I'm beginning to think are a compulsory accessory of B&Bs – bound out to meet us. They are followed by the hostess, Mally Francis, who emerges from her detached studio, where she paints minutely detailed pictures of plants and flowers with the botanical exactitude of Banks or Solander and prints them as greeting cards.

She takes to the task of running a B&B with the same sort of attention to aesthetic detail. The table linen is a William Morris floral, the breakfast jams home-made. Traces of expensive scents – more like perfume than air freshener, as though a housemaid might have wandered through seconds ago with a bunch of freshly picked flowers – linger in the corridors. A small basket in each bathroom contains full-sized (not motel-tiny) dispensers of Marks and Spencer's toiletries. The bed linen is Egyptian cotton.

'What a lovely woman,' Mum enthuses as we unpack. 'She said they thought I was an Englishwoman. I felt quite flattered.'

It's too late to visit the gardens, so we head for the pub in the nearby village of St Ewe. The Crown Inn, its frontage dressed resplendently in hanging flower baskets, opens directly onto the street. Only a wide expanse of waste ground behind, that serves as an unsealed car park, attests to the fact that Heligan delivers it more custom than is normal for a small hostelry.

The grizzled landlord, John Nelson, turns out to know a bit about the gardens. He's an easy talker, and chuckling consumptively, he keeps an eye on proceedings from the end of the bar, showing diners to their tables and discussing the menu with gruff good humour.

The pub is crowded with diners. The waiting staff constantly working the three dozen tables must be familiar with who's starting and who's nearly finished, but they all report to the landlord and ask 'Have you got a four, John?' or 'Can you do us a two in 10 minutes?' It's all part of the role he plays – part mine host and part lord of the manor.

Between these frequent interruptions, he sips his pint, tugs on a cigarette, which spends much of its time burning in the ashtray, and, creasing his weathered features into a grinning squint, looks back down the years at the making of Heligan.

The garden, he explains, was uncovered by pulling away 70 years' worth of weeds.

'You seem to know a lot about it,' I say.

He smiles, takes another drag on his cigarette and jerks a thumb over his shoulder at a large framed photograph on the wall that shows him next to a smiling Prince Charles at the gardens' official opening. He looks funny in a suit.

'It was just me and the dog for the first 18 months,' he says. 'I'd known about this place for 40 years, but it wasn't until I started cutting into it that I began to realise how it was all still there, perfectly preserved and waiting to be uncovered.'

There have been gardens at Heligan since the late sixteenth century. The Tremaynes, whose ancestral seat is in the gardens' centre, created plots of both produce and beauty for their own use. As the years went by they developed an extraordinary garden, which showcased the revolutionary horticultural technologies of the Victorian era.

But then, explains Nelson, came the twentieth century. 'Two world wars. All the gardeners went to war and the gardens were run down.'

Helped by volunteers from a national conservation trust, Nelson and his dog cleared more than seven decades' worth of growth in a year. They were grateful for the old gardeners' practice of spreading sea salt on the paths to keep the weeds down.

'We could peel the creepers back like a carpet and usually we would find paths and drains in perfect condition.'

Now the site, which covers almost 200 hectares, showcases

every conceivable kind of horticultural husbandry: precisely planted vegetable gardens and tonsured lawns; melon and fig houses and a pineapple pit; herbariums and hedges, shrubberies, rockeries and areas of woodland wild enough to earn the name 'jungle', although a Brazilian might find a more Amazonian atmosphere on a Rio de Janeiro apartment balcony.

There's even a place called New Zealand. No one seems able to explain the nineteenth-century gardeners' fascination with our end of the world, but it was plainly profound. One of the few photographs of that era – an 1890s shot, which is the frontispiece to the enterprise's official history – shows the head gardener all done out in his Sunday best, waist-deep in a pool of silver-grey fern.

The small imported patch is not that impressive to any Kiwi who has done a bit of bushwalking. But it is still an eerie feeling to come upon a slice of New Zealand native bush in the middle of the Cornish Riviera. Here a new totara glows silver in the gloom cast by tree ferns. There the clusters of yellow-green starburst announce a cabbage tree (never mind that they call it a Torbay Cornish palm). In the lower growth, fuchsias wink. Grasses – silver-grey or straw-black – line the rocky path edges.

The Cornish weather seems to agree with our flora. In this patch are several kinds of kowhai, large forget-me-nots from the Chathams, rengarenga lily, clematis, oddly shaped pittosporums, muehlenbeckia and tree ferns which came as ballast on ships from Australia.

I am expecting Mum to be transported by the experience but she seems mildly unimpressed. She tells me that she was expecting more colour, particularly since it's the middle of summer. She has certainly earned the right to pass judgement, having spent at least a few hours each week of her life in the garden, breaking in several sections from scratch to create rockeries and orchards and shrubberies and flower beds.

Dad was the dilettante of the pair who maintained the rose beds Mum dug, and cultivated orchids, which he spoke of in hushed tones although they looked faintly tatty most of the time. He would bring successful blooms inside and stand them conspicuously in a sherry glass. We were all meant to admire them but I hated the way the blooms jutted at odd angles from the stem. They looked faintly malevolent, reminding me of triffids or the fabled flesh-eating plants of Amazonia and not at all of the symmetrical smiling flowers of my childish drawing.

Dad would spend Saturday afternoons mixing up odd potions to spray the aphids on the roses – he loved recalling how one of us boys once asked him whether he was spraying 'to kill the atheists'. But Mum did the hard work – the unrewarding, constant, backbreaking toil.

Mum says that gardening has always been 'my therapy' – the place where she could work out her frustrations and anxieties. But it's a palliative she resorts to less and less these days. For the last 10 years every conversation I've ever had with her has contained the sighing phrase 'I've got to get out in the garden.' But when she does – or when I find her at work in the garden – it seems like a battle. Gardening always seems to be a series of unmanageable challenges to be surmounted – hedges that need trimming, vast expanses of steep lawn to be mowed and weeds, rampant after rain, to be pulled.

As age has wearied her, so it has dulled her pleasure and much of her gardening is accomplished these days by the very sensible expedient of 'getting a man in'.

I had thought she would regard a visit to Heligan as a Muslim might regard being dropped off at Mecca but I can understand her reservation. It is a wonderful achievement, a sort of living museum of horticultural practice, but my strongest feeling – even in the New Zealand part – is that I am in an alien landscape. Laurens van der Post once wrote that we can only fall in love with one landscape and I realise with an agreeable start that this could never be mine.

Yet ours was not a New Zealand garden. No one ever dug potatoes for dinner or washed a freshly picked lettuce under the kitchen tap. We grew potatoes once, an entire section full of them, but it was only to break up the soil so that Dad might plant a golf-green-perfect lawn of Chewings' fescue. I think the crop was given – or even thrown – away.

My parents never had a vegetable garden in my lifetime –

though they did in their early, impoverished married life. I once dug a small patch behind the garage and sprinkled radish seeds with uneducated profusion. The seeds were given to me by one or other indulgent parent on the grounds that radishes are virtually impossible to fail to grow. Shortly the little square of roughly tilled clods was a forest of radishes and, remembering I hated radishes, I returned the garden to lawn by passing the mower over it a couple of times.

So for Mum, the gardening was hard work and for Dad, it was faintly aristocratic dabbling. Though I would never describe Dad as a dabbler in his professional life or musical pursuits, he was always a dilettante gardener, but at least he seemed to gain pleasure from it.

I watch Mum inspecting the vegetable gardens at Heligan. The expression on her face recalls the Queen inspecting an honour guard. I find myself wondering whether she truly, deeply, enjoyed anything about her life.

I spoke to her about that on our last night together in London, in the Spanish restaurant in Bayswater. We were talking about an old family friend, Jimmy Stimpson, who had courted Mum before she met Dad. He was 15 years older and 'had an eye for the ladies' she recalled. 'He tried to kiss me one night and I would have let him except for the fact that he had the most dreadful breath.'

Jimmy was a frequent visitor to our house as I grew up, a charming and very correct Englishman. Perhaps he imperfectly disguised his disappointment that he had missed out on Mum, or perhaps Mum alluded to it during dark times. Certainly I was always dimly aware of the spark between them. I noticed the way he called her 'Joanie' or 'darling' and the sadness that passed like a cloud across his face at times when they were together and Dad was away.

The most fascinating thing about him was that he had an artificial leg. He'd lost his own in a motorcycle accident – his passion for big, loud bikes was another thing that terrified my ingénue mother. I never tired of the thrill of horror I would get from sneaking into his room early in the morning and seeing the disembodied limb, leaning in the corner or lying on the floor. I always felt there was something desperately sad about the neatly laced shoe on the end of it, its uppers uncreased by the sole's flexion, its sock forever freshly laundered.

'He was a lovely man,' Mum recalled, 'and very anxious after we met to see that I was happy.'

We can't leave Cornwall before visiting an achievement even more astounding than Heligan. The Eden Project, which opened in May 2001, was the brainchild of Tim Smit who partnered John Nelson at the lost gardens. 'He did all the talking and I did all the work,' says Nelson, without a trace of rancour, which is not surprising since Smit's talking raised all the money.

A giant disused china clay quarry near St Austell in Cornwall has been landscaped into what its creators are touting as the eighth wonder of the world. The Eden Project is more than a garden, more even than a collection of giant greenhouses, called biomes, which are the most striking sight when you arrive at the edge of the 15-hectare crater. It calls itself 'a theatre in which to tell the story of human dependence on plants'.

The sheer numbers beggar belief: Smit, his credibility assured by the achievement at Heligan, raised almost NZ$300 million from public and private sources to build it. They moved 1.8 million tonnes of soil out and 100,000 tonnes of compost in to make a new Eden in what was once a clay wasteland.

The centrepieces are the enormous geodesic domes, made of more than 360 kilometres of scaffolding covered with a space-age transparent foil. The resulting biomes contain two indoor environments – one tropical and one temperate – and a third, uncovered one in which grow more than 4000 plants from all over the world.

The idea is that Eden should be a living encyclopaedia of the plants humans have used – whether for food, medicine, building or weaving – and a living institute designed to educate people about the relationship between the human and plant worlds.

It's a hugely impressive achievement, built in the face of great challenges – not least a two-month downpour in the early stages of construction, which dumped more than 160 million litres of water into the pit.

I trundle Mum round the wheelchair-friendly paths and up ramps in and out of the biomes, marvelling at the profusion of landscapes, from Amazonia to Arizona. Faced with an uphill slog out of the enormous pit and back to the car I decide to head for the tractor-drawn train that ferries visitors up. I'm amazed at the length of the queue, which comprises mainly able-bodied folk who could easily make the five-minute ascent on foot. Instead they wait, in an orderly line, for what looks like it will be half an hour in the hot sun.

It's a curiosity of the English that, faced with the option of doing something or queuing, they will always elect to stand in line. The Hungarian-born humorist George Mikes noticed it when he went to England, where he spent his adult life.

'A man in a queue,' he wrote in the hilarious *How to Be Inimitable*, 'is as much the image of a true Briton as a man in a bullring is the image of a Spaniard or a man with a two-foot cigar of an American.' And in *To Be an Alien*: 'An Englishman, even if he is alone, forms an orderly queue of one.'

I can't help staring in wonder as I look at the lines of gawping Brits treating Mikes' humorous observations as an instruction manual. They stand silently and in a fashion so orderly that it's chilling.

I've spent hours – and on one visit three days – in Latin America waiting for scheduled transport services to arrive or depart. Ditto in Asia. They know what queuing is in those parts of the world. You mill and surge, which is something accomplished only by concerted action. It's impossible to do on your own. But battling on alone is the British way.

The line is so long I am about to attempt the ascent on foot, pushing Mum – who is warming to the wheelchair as a mode of transport – ahead of me. But suddenly a uniformed man at the head of the queue is beckoning.

''Ere you are, sir,' he calls, and the queue shuffles to one side as I roll Mother to the head of it.

'There's one just leaving now, sir,' the attendant says, 'but that's full. We'll get you and Mum on the next one.'

'I'm perfectly capable of walking,' Mum begins to say but I drown her out with a bellowed, 'That's very kind of you.' He moves away with a smile and I bend to explain to Mother the virtue of silence.

JUST TO BE HERE

We're heading for Land's End, for no good reason other than that it is there. We want to retrace the route followed by Henry and Priscilla White when they left Penzance for Plymouth in 1842 to board the *Westminster* for New Zealand. But it makes no sense to travel the same road in reverse so we have decided to start at the finish.

As we streak along Cornwall's backbone, the A30, I realise why the most south-western county is so often referred to as a beautiful frame around a plain picture. The coastline is breath-taking, even for a Kiwi who knows Westland or Kaikoura or the Coromandel. But the countryside, bare, even bleak, is largely treeless, and undulates so that the horizon leaps into view only at moments, when the car crests the swell of the land. Much of the time we wallow in the troughs, where the pitch and toss of the heathered hillsides is faintly menacing.

Mum's feeling fretful, although she doesn't realise it. It leaks from around the edges of the sighing pronouncements from the passenger seat where she sits, hands folded, and worries about what she's missing. Most of her sentences begin with the words 'It's just a pity that …'

Like most things in her life – like most things in everyone's life – the trip has been starkly different from the fantasy, nurtured through a thousand excited nights as she lay going to sleep. In dreams, she picked her way through the past at leisure, taking the time earned by a lifetime of hard work. Her husband was at her side. They held hands at times, spoke of the near past as they looked over the distant one. When they came to a village they liked, they stayed a night, maybe two, walking the same stretch of beach or sitting in a damp, shady churchyard more than once, and savouring the way it tasted different each time.

In reality, she is being bustled along like a dawdling and errant schoolchild. She tries hard to enjoy it, exploding with delight when a churchyard leaps into view, filled with mossy grey headstones, or when the thatched roofs of a village peep over the willows that shield it from the rushing road: 'Look at that!' she will cry. 'Those are the things I like to see. Look at the *age* of that tree!'

I think for a moment of Tane Mahuta glowering in the forest south of the Hokianga while Britons were running round in bearskins and sleeping in caves. I say nothing. Mum is moving through a world whose age charms her and connects her to it. Through the window of the twenty-first century rental car, she can gaze on the landscape and fancy herself as home at last, far from a brash, rough, young country devoid of history and back in the land where she belongs.

The age of everything is her constant delight. Through London and the south the cobblestoned streets are another favourite, even though most of them are no older than the streets of Auckland – out the back of His Majesty's perhaps – where she walked as a young woman. The paving stones, chipped and ground under horses' hooves and wagon wheels, are among history's most expendable resources. We antipodeans are fond of stroking the ground of the old country, even if only metaphorically, and imagining that we touch the ground that was brushed by the feet of figures from our history books. But we forget that those roads have long been worn away by the passage of time.

'You really are wonderful, you know,' she says, 'to do all this for me.'

Then she sighs and adds, 'We can't expect to do everything,' and not for the first time, I grip the steering wheel so my knuckles whiten.

'I wish you'd stop that,' I snap.

'Stop what?' she asks, looking to see if perhaps the hem of her dress has draped over the gearstick.

'Sighing and saying you wish you were doing something else!'

'I don't wish I were doing something else, dear,' she says. 'I'm perfectly happy just sitting here and looking out the window.'

I'm feeling irritated – and, worse, angry with myself for being irritated – at her discontent.

'Everything you say,' I persist, like a driver who accelerates as the looming cliff edge gets nearer, 'seems saturated with such disappointment. Every sentence begins with "It's a pity that …" It's very disconcerting.'

'I'm not disappointed at all, dear,' she says in a disappointed-sounding voice. 'I'm only saying that we couldn't possibly hope to cover the ground that Geoff covered. He was here for months. And anyway he came twice.'

'What ground aren't we covering that he covered?' I demand. I'm like a fox, keen enough to scent blood but too stupid to realise that it's his own.

'Nothing in particular,' she says, defensively. 'This is all I want. Just to look. Just to feel. The *age* of everything.'

Dimly sensing I've been outwitted, I flick on the indicator and pull left. The exit for Penzance is just ahead.

These are just names now, of course. I've combed them out of the pages of Geoff's book, *Of Toffs and Toilers*, a family history inspired by his travels in Cornwall and Lancashire where he sniffed his past out like an amateur sleuth. His wanderings in the south-west had taken him to Gulval, near Penzance, where Henry and Priscilla White, Mum's great-grandparents, had married on July 22, 1837.

It's not hard for us to find the church; it is beyond the graveyard, which sulks in the damp shade. The ground has heaved and swollen around the gravestones, which lean at drunken angles, and we emerge from the gloom of the pathway into a yard bathed in brief sunlight. The door, unusually for a small village church, is locked; so Mum sits on a bench near the door, gazing about her and trying to breathe in the atmosphere.

'I don't really need to see their names in the parish register,' she says at last, sounding like someone who dearly wanted to see their names in the parish register. Geoff had observed that one of the witnesses at the wedding had signed the register with 'only her mark … as, like most of her generation, she had been without schooling'. I could tell Mum longed to see that mark, to trace it with hands scarred by a lifetime of work, to touch her past. But the church is locked. The process of bringing the records into the light of day would anyway be long-winded and complicated, something best arranged months in advance; and time is short. I snap off a shot of Mum on the hard bench.

I grind my teeth and feel bowed by a sense of failure that this trip, like so much of Mum's life, is a second-best experience. Even though I've told her she couldn't expect exactly to mimic Geoff's trips – he'd come twice, after all, and spent several weeks down here alone – I feel like the child I am. I am reminded, suddenly, absurdly, of the cheap pipes we used to buy Dad at Christmas and the eloquent delight he displayed even though he knew they would be unsmokeable. I want her to be delighted, too, though more sophisticatedly, so I am convinced the way I used to be then. But in her faintly disappointed reaction to everything I feel I can see the future: a return to New Zealand where she will sit, her back to the view from her lounge, and regret that it hadn't been some other way.

But here I am, pushing her through her past with something approaching indecent haste. I know that Penzance is the epicentre of her pilgrimage but our itinerary has us staying far from here, near St Austell. Penzance, the main event, is a long day trip.

Still I try to make the best of it. As we make our way back to the car, parked in the sleepy square in the middle of the cluster of houses that is Gulval, a man walking his dog passes and I ask after Chyandour where Henry, Mum's grandfather was born in 1839. I pronounce it in three syllables as if it were a French name, 'She-on-dour' and it takes a second or two for him to realise what I'm talking about.

'Ar, Chai-endower,' he says, cheerfully, chewing on the final 'r' as though it were toffee. 'You follow this road here down to the bottom till you hit the seaside and you're there.'

I follow his directions carefully, but at the bottom there is no sign that there is any 'there' there at all. The ribbon of houses running along the seafront seems inseparable from Penzance barely 200 metres further on.

I drive onto the docks and ask a corpulent cab driver. He swivels, none too willingly, in his seat and peers back the way we've come.

'You see that white house with the red roof?' he says. 'That's it.'

'The house …?'

'That's it.'

'… is Chyandour?'

'That's it.'

'I thought it was a village.'

'Well, it is a village.'

'But you said the house …?' I protest.

'Well, the 'ouse ain't Chyandour,' he says, looking at me pityingly. 'But that's where Chyandour is.'

'In the house,' I say. Well, I don't really. By this time I realise that Chyandour hasn't been a distinct village for at least half a century. It's just a stretch of road. I thank the cabbie and head back to the car.

'Did you find it,' Mum asks.

'I did,' I reply. 'You see that white house with the red roof?'

'The house …?'

'That's it.'

'… is Chyandour?'

'That's it.'

'I thought it was a village.'

'Well, it is a village. We'll look at it on the way back.'

We drive through Penzance, snatching glimpses down the streets with evocative names like Market Jew Street, and before I know what's happened I'm on the road for Land's End. I pull off onto a road that snakes along the seafront and park. I ask Mum what she wants to see.

'Anything you like, dear,' she says, peering myopically through her dark glasses at the whitewashed houses. 'Look at those sweet little houses.'

'It's not a matter of what I like,' I explode. 'It's your trip.'

The words are barely out before I realise how stupid, not to say unfair, they are. It may be Mum's last chance to be here, but I am refusing to admit the trip is a pilgrimage of my own. I feel an unreasoning rage that she hasn't swotted up in advance and made a list of all the places she wants to see.

'Just to be here, dear,' she says, but all I can hear is the dismissive 'just'. Disconsolately I start the car and head for Land's End.

Travellers love extremities, one assumes, the way they love superlatives. They beat a path to the tallest or deepest or oldest even when others of the kind are more accessible or beautiful. As a result, of course, they end up shoulder-to-shoulder with crowds they could easily have avoided.

Land's End is no more or less beautiful than the rest of the Cornish coast in the vicinity. But on this hot, late August afternoon it heaves with humanity. I begin to sense that we've made a mistake as I pass hordes of people, most of them propelled by hairless and impossibly white English legs, walking the last couple of kilometres from the 'free parking'. It costs nothing to visit the most westerly point in Britain but it costs £3 to park the car.

I brace myself to appeal to the ticket-taker's better nature, on the grounds that I have an elderly travelling companion and that most precious journalist's *vade mecum*, a letter from the local tourist authority. But the young man in the ticket booth gives the letter – and my passenger – barely a glance. He's more interested in my accent.

'Rotorua, originally,' he says, 'but I've been living in Christchurch.' I should have picked him immediately, if not as a Kiwi, at least as an antipodean, from the way he slouches shirtless and leans back on his high stool with his jandal-stained feet wedged against the booth's narrow counter. In an unquestioning gesture of national solidarity he waves me through with a cheerful 'No worries' and we park in the disabled space right next to the buildings.

The *Lonely Planet* has warned that the place is 'a Thatcherite monument to the triumph of crass commerce over culture', which doubtless explains its popularity. A cluster of buildings houses exhibits with expensive entry fees, including Miles of Memories, which records the many ways – including, presumably, cricketer Ian Botham's famously foot-blistering, vodka-fuelled walk for charity – of getting from Land's End to

John o'Groat's. Overdressed tourists stand and gawp as ice cream trickles down their sleeves. Buskers blare.

I look around and Mum has disappeared. I spend long, exasperated minutes looking for her in the throng and finally decide to abandon her and trek the 200 metres or so down to the end without her. But my moment of high-handed triumph is short-lived. I emerge from the courtyard to the sight of her waving her stick to attract my attention.

'There you are,' she says, as if I, not she, were lost. I sigh.

The path to the land's end snakes through heather, which is just beginning its late-summer purple bloom. The headland is crowded. I thrust the camera into the hands of an innocent bystander, practically demanding that she shoot a picture. I have it still and it seems like an emblem of the trip, or of that day of it anyway. Hidden behind dark glasses and under a shapeless white floppy, I scowl; Mum looks faintly bemused, as if wondering what on earth we're doing here.

But it's the afternoon now and we still have the family trail to follow. Beyond the town we cruise past the red-roofed house which purports to be Chyandour not once but three times, whipping around traffic islands to retrace our steps, and struggling to make some nineteenth-century sense of landscape now sliced with six-lane arterial roads. They would have been mud and chalky clay when Henry and Priscilla traversed them, making their last journey on English soil all those years ago. Geoff travelled this road, too, but with an explorer's sense of purpose and I pause in my self-indulgent grumbling for a moment to thank him for the record he left us.

'The party of 13,' he wrote, 'gathered a few mornings earlier to load the carrier's cart. It took essentials only, piled around spaces left for the smaller children. The others had to walk alongside unless the horses found the going easy.'

Much of what follows is evocative speculation, but it's not hard to imagine that it's accurate. 'Friends and neighbours stood about chatting,' he goes on, 'perhaps secretly wishing they too had the courage to take the same bold steps. Some were members of the Wesleyan Chapel in Chapel Street, where the next meeting recorded that 'the Whites and the Daveys got away at last'.

'The horses took the strain, drawing the load through the town, past the Market House, along Market Jew Street, across the Gulval flat [where, I imagine, they had no trouble at all identifying Chyandour, even without the assistance of a taxi driver] and up the hill to Marazion.'

Mum is reading from the book as we drive. 'The sturdy stone of St Michael's Mount lay in the wide bay and Penzance became dim behind.'

Geoff concludes that the trip 'across the Kenneggy Downs above Prussia Cove, through Breage and on to Helston' would have 'completed the first day'. It takes us a few minutes, hissing along the highway on new tyres in light rain as Radio Four coos quietly on the four-speaker stereo.

But it is not just our speed and comfort that makes it hard for us to have any sense of the journey. The landscape the Whites and Daveys crossed is unrecognisable now, dramatically different even from what Geoff saw and wrote about in the 1970s. Time and again I pull over, trying to make sense of it for Mum, who is struggling to suppress a slightly panicky feeling that the reason for our being here at all is receding in the rear-view mirror. Perhaps that is where all history is for us, travellers in a hurry as we are. Only now as I write, do I realise that we should have walked the streets of Penzance, to stand outside the chapel where they loaded the cart, to walk along Market Jew Street where the rattle of the wheels on the cobbles drowned out the cheers of their well-wishers and the storm of anxiety in their hearts.

I pull out onto the road again, keen to make good time, desperate to make good sense. But time has stripped the landscape rushing by of the magic Geoff saw and recorded as he retraced the route of the Whites and Daveys. The names drip with poetic resonance, exotic even though – or perhaps because – they are so deeply buried in our shared genetic memory: the Wendron Moors, the valley of the Fal, the great Carrick Roads, Truro, Probus, St Austell, Lostwithiel (looking through twentieth-century eyes, Geoff calls it 'pretty' though its prettiness would probably have escaped the anxious and apprehensive travellers).

I find myself charmed by the cadences of the names and wonder why it would not be the same if they were New Zealand place names.

'Across the Fowey,' he has them travelling 'with bleak Bodmin Moor to the north as Liskeard came nearer.' And the list goes on. Trefule Foot, Polbathic, Sheviock, 'then downhill through the tight-packed cottages of Torpoint into the yard of the London Inn in Ferry Street.

'The *Westminster* lay out towards Kingsand and Cawsand, hidden around the point in the wider sound. The final morning came with the punted crossing and the short journey to the Plymouth Quay. It was December 4, 1842.'

As we wind along the B-roads near the coast, I realise that this is more than simply a description of what he saw. It's a road map for future generations, a list of directions they must follow.

The landscape the Daveys and Whites looked at through frightened eyes is buried now beneath new housing estates. The car eats up the wet roads, joining the dots of the frequent roundabouts that punctuate our progress. We whisk briskly past villages which, then, would have been waypoints on the Whites' last anxious journey on English soil.

As I watch the road signs pass, all pointing left or right to places we were missing, I find myself imagining what it must have been like and talking in a low and sentimental voice to Mum, trying to conjure up the images for her.

The horse-drawn cart would have laboured up muddied slopes and rattled through what passed for main streets. Behind it, the adults and older children would have walked, the women holding their skirts up from the grime. They would have smiled wanly at the curious faces of those who watched them pass.

No one notices our progress and the afternoon is catching up with us. Long before Plymouth I turn back, heading for the lodgings at Heligan again.

Our adventure in the south-west is at an end and I can barely bring myself to look at Mum. All the months of planning, the years of postponement, the battles against decrepitude and injury should have left me feeling a sense of triumph and achievement. I am not used to travelling like this, tyrannised by a timetable, denied the chance to detour or retrace our steps. I feel an unreasoning sense of rage towards Mum for not having been more specific about what she wanted to see and do. But to the extent that we have failed, I am responsible. Having upended the parent-child relationship, having bossed her into the trip and then bossed her through it, I had failed to realise that I needed to design it for her, questioning her about her needs and wants as an architect might question a client, to extract from her intelligence of desires she never even knew she had.

We leave for Truro in plenty of time to drop off the car at the hire firm's office at the station. I am hoping they won't notice the small scuffing of the wing mirror, administered by a passing van in a narrow lane in Devon before I learned to fold them in on the tightest stretches of road. In the event, they barely have time to. Not once, but twice I miss the turn-off to the station and we arrive in a hail of skidded stones. I dispatch Mum, limping and muttering, in the direction of the platform – two long, panting staircases and an overbridge away on the other side of the tracks. Then I positively drag the mystified young attendant on a cursory inspection before throwing the keys at her and hollering over my retreating shoulder that she can send the paperwork to me in New Zealand.

After all that, predictably enough, the train is late, and we wait several minutes in the sweltering heat. Our tickets entitle us to a seat in first class, which is normally at the front of the train; but when we haul ourselves aboard we find they've assembled the line of wagons in reverse order and we're in a crowded second-class carriage. When I turn to disembark and drag Mum and her small suitcase along the platform to the right carriage, I find our way barred by a lanky, spotty-faced uniformed youth who insists the train is about to leave and that there is no time for us to change carriages. We battle and jostle our way the full length of the train, through aisles a critical centimetre or two too narrow for Mum's modest cabin-bag-sized trolley case. Fat Englishmen clutter the aisle, sometimes with their seal-sleek cream-bun bodies, other times with suitcases that almost completely block our progress. When I ask them to move their luggage they respond by rolling their eyes long-sufferingly heavenwards and clicking their tongues disapprovingly and I find myself calculating my chances of delivering a king hit in such a confined space.

The heat – and my ill temper – build in parallel until we reach our own seats, after several long minutes of hauling and crawling. The train has yet to leave. I thrust my head out the door looking for our weedy and officious porter but he's nowhere to be seen.

Back in London, we take a cab to a hotel in nearby Bayswater. The dismissive Frenchman on the desk hands us our key and points us down a corridor behind the desk. This, it turns out, leads to a windowless room barely larger than a couple of single beds beside a cleaning cupboard in the very bowels of the hotel. I return to the desk to remonstrate with him. He greets the news that my mother is 81 not to mention travel-sore with an indifferent Gallic shrug, which seems to suggest that we all have to die sometime, and pokes desultorily at his keyboard before allocating us another room on the third floor. This is reached by a lift with a mind of its own. It descends when instructed to ascend and the door remains closed when we reach our stop until I work out that I need to press the 'Door Open' button. But after a corridor full of two-step staircases and tight corners, we land up at last in a room that features a double window to the sunny street and an ancient device that presses your trousers overnight.

We repair to the bar for a spirit-reviving drink, only to find it is closed. It's 5.30 p.m., which is not, it seems to me, a wholly unreasonable time to expect a drink in a hotel; but the porter who stands smilingly behind it tells us that the barman is not due to start work until 6 p.m.

'I can make you a beer,' he says, in a thick Spanish accent, pointing at an array of cans in the glass-fronted fridge behind him.

'Well, why don't you make me a beer,' I say slowly, 'and

make my mother a gin and tonic.'

'A geen and tonica,' he says, mulling over the request slowly as if I have asked him to sequence the DNA of a banana. 'The barman does not start until …'

'Yes, I know what time the barman starts,' I reply. 'Do you see that bottle there? That's gin. What you do is you bang a bit of that in a glass …' I break off, aware that he is smiling indulgently at me as though I were a cretin.

'I am sorry, sir,' he says, sounding not very sorry at all, 'but the barman …'

I turn to Mum, who is wilting thirstily on an armchair behind me.

'Would you like a beer, Mum?'

'Whatever you like, dear,' she says. 'A gin and tonic would be nice.'

We eat later at a Spanish restaurant two doors away. The family-run establishment is cheerful and, by London standards, cheap. It follows the civilised continental habit of bringing a bottle of wine to the table and charging you only for the proportion of it that you consume. We'll just have a couple of glasses, I think. But as the evening wears on, the level of wine in the bottle drops.

I ask her about the trip, how much she's enjoyed it.

'It's been lovely, dear. You've been wonderful.'

'Have you liked it here?'

'I love it here,' she says. 'I wish, in many ways, that I had been born in England. I wish I had been born English. Because it's in my blood and yet it's not. I'm of the soil, my blood is English, but I'm just an ordinary common-or-garden New Zealander and I resent that in a certain fashion.

'It's not a matter of not being proud of being a New Zealander, but this is why I'm so strongly against New Zealand ever becoming a republic – because we are British. In spite of the way we treated the Maori that's the way lands were conquered. People went overseas and they claimed lands for the dominions beyond the seas. Britannia rules the waves.

'I suppose I would like to have lived in one of those little villages and walked down to the shops with my kit over my arm. Hamilton is so ordinary to me. I'm English to the core and I wish that I had been born in England.'

STRANGER IN A STRANGE LAND

David and Margaret arrive early to collect Mum. We have barely returned to the hotel from cashing a traveller's cheque – a gruelling, limping walk (Mum refuses to take a taxi) to the nearest branch of Lloyds to avoid the exchange booths on the Bayswater Road, where they extract a swingeing 10 per cent commission.

They drive us back to Soho to where we left our luggage and then to the house in Camden Town where I plan to spend the next few weeks. No one is home so I leave my bags with a neighbour and we head over to Hampstead to the house, on the edge of the heath, where David spent his early years. It's a stolid, square Georgian box of four unadorned storeys, which his mother bought in the early fifties for £5000 and which is now worth more than £8 million. Its owner is 'Lord Something or Other' David tells me. It seems as far as might be imagined from the dusty corner in Tramway Road where the bully girls tormented me.

We have lunch and a pint at an old pub and David walks me up the hill to Jack Straw's Castle. I had been expecting some stately home occupied by the Home Secretary, who was famous for his campaign to get 'tough on crime, tough on the causes of crime', but it's not that Jack Straw at all, as it turns out. It's a pub – which looks rather like a beached Mississippi riverboat – named after another Jack Straw, the one who led a peasant's revolt in the fourteenth century. In later years, the gibbeted bodies of highwaymen would rot in chains here. The pub, or an earlier incarnation of it, was a favourite of the novelist Charles Dickens, who once wrote to a friend, 'You don't feel disposed, do you, to muffle yourself and start off with me for a brisk walk over Hampstead Heath? I know a good house where we can have a red-hot chop for dinner.'

High on the hill, looking over the heath, it is time to say goodbye to Mum, and I feel suddenly, inexplicably, bereft. It is not that I don't want to hand her over. A devotee of solo travel, I've been looking forward to this moment for some time, but it seems full of sadness, of a sense that somehow it hasn't been what I wanted it to be. The months of planning, the frustrations of delay, the quiet triumph of watching our carefully constructed plans come to fruition, it's all over now. I had thought it would be unendurable, but it all seems to have flashed by in a blur and all I can think of are the opportunities missed, the gap between the dreams I had of a woman transformed as she touches her past and the messy, slightly gruelling reality of ticking off items on an itinerary or following the suggestions of a guidebook. I know Mum feels something the same but she is not letting on.

'Goodbye, son,' she says quietly and the choice of the word 'son' rather than the normal 'dear' is the only clue to how she is feeling: maternal. But she throws her arms around me and whispers, 'You've been a champion,' in my ear.

'Bye, dear,' I say, embracing her briefly. 'Have a good time up north. I'll come and see you in a couple of weeks.'

I shake hands with David, kiss Margaret's cheek and with that I am gone, down into the heath and across to where I am staying.

The owners – a colleague of my wife, and her husband – are very welcoming, but their house is in turmoil. I install myself in their sunlit, airy, attic space, which is accessed by a steep ladder and well away from the disaster area below. They have just bought the house and moved in, accompanied by a cheerful trio of decorators – all Kiwis – who are redoing everything. The figures defy belief. The house is about 6 metres wide – though it has four floors and five bedrooms if you count the attic and seems quite roomy – but it cost £560,000, which at the ruinous prevailing exchange rate is the best part of $2 million. The workmen are likely to swallow up another £50,000.

Alone at last, I become aware of the low-level anxiety that has been chewing away at me for the last 10 days. It's hard to settle down, to accept that I only have to watch out for myself when I cross the street.

A well-connected friend has arranged a ticket to a premiership football game – Arsenal are at home to West Bromwich Albion – and I take the bus down Tufnell Park Road towards Holloway Road and the club's home ground at Finsbury Park. It's not hard to find the way. The street is a slowly moving sea of people, crested here and there by unsmiling mounted policemen with stout batons and stouter walkie-talkies attached to their belts.

I thought I had left enough time for a meal, which I had planned, foolishly it turns out, to have at a pub. But the only pubs along the crowded street are heaving with drinkers, who spill out onto the pavement clutching pint glasses – plastic ones, doubtless to minimise their potential as weapons. Instead, I attach myself to the end of a queue that loops into and out of a chippie.

The man standing next to me is elderly – about Mum's age, I guess – but lean and sinewy. He flashes me a toothless smile. His eyes are moon-huge behind the lenses of his industrial-strength spectacles. His long red-and-white scarf proclaims his allegiance to the home team. His name is Bob.

'So, who d'you fancy, then?' I ask, somewhat superfluously.

'Gunners,' Bob says and the large eyes sparkle through the rheum. (The team's nickname, like its name, is a reminder of its origin as a works side from a long-closed armaments factory).

'You come to all the games?'

It turns out he does, making the three-hour return trip on the train from Portsmouth. He proudly brandishes his season ticket – which has cost him the cut-rate pensioner's price of £850.

'Where you from, then?' he asks and shakes his head when I explain to him that where I come from 'football' means rugby union.

'Bloody toffs' game, that, innit?' he growls and is only slightly pacified when I add that league – a working-class northerners' game in England – is popular, too.

Sensing that I may have strayed into dangerous territory, I change the subject and admire his scarf.

'I was thinking of getting some sort of souvenir,' I say. 'Will they have stalls on the way to the ground?'

'What yew want, then?' he asks.

'A scarf, maybe. Maybe just a rattle. Do they still have rattles?'

I have hardly finished the sentence before he removes his scarf and puts it around my neck with the reverence of a Tibetan Buddhist welcoming the Dalai Lama.

'There y'are,' he says. 'You got one now.'

'You can't do that,' I protest feebly, overwhelmed by his gesture.

'I just have, haven't I,' he says and the queue starts moving.

The scarf, it turns out, is a memento of the Gunners' victory (over Newcastle) in the 1998 FA Cup. Even a soccer sceptic from the other side of the world can sense that he has been gifted something close to a holy relic.

It adds spice to the evening, although I feel like a bit of a fraud wearing the red-and-white. It marks me out as a member of a club I could never belong to. As the tide of fans sweeps down the streets, I am carried along, a foreign piece of flotsam in the surge of local passion.

The world over, football is an index of culture. The meaning of the word itself changes according to the language or accent in which it is spoken. To most of the world – almost every country between the meridians of longitude that run through Chile and as far east as, say, Turkey, football means what I grew up calling soccer. But it means something special in Melbourne; the world might call the oval-field game they play 'Australian rules' but Victorians – and, for that matter – the footy fans of South and Western Australia – call it football. In our neck of the woods, football is the 15-man game at which – in days I can still remember as though they were yesterday – the All Blacks were the undisputed champions.

But in the *favelas* of Rio and the dusty streets of central Africa, in the steep cobbled alleys of Umbria, and here, on the choking streets of Finsbury Park, football is football. To say that it long ago replaced religion as the opiate of the masses seems obvious, but I had never come face to face with the reality of the English passion for the game. There's an almost palpable sense in the street that the whole week has been lived through – endured even – for this 90 minutes. Match night is what makes life worth living.

Inside the stadium, the players glide across the immaculately groomed greener-than-real turf, which has been mown into a perfectly regular chequer board. Stationed behind the goal but well up in the stand, I struggle to pay attention to the match: the fans, engaged in their alien liturgy, seem more interesting than the on-field action. The punters' nationality seems to define them less than their passion for the game. They seem, on this night at least, to have more in common with the Argentinians I once shared stadium seats with in Buenos Aires than with me, even though I come from something like the same genetic stock.

In Argentina, the fans crowded behind tall fences with reels of razor wire at top and bottom, human seas surging and boiling. The undulations of the crowd resembled nothing so much as a landscape tortured by earthquake. Here it is much the same. As day gives way to night and the stadium lights burn brighter, the full-throated enthusiasm of the fans builds, a parody of melody designed simply to drown out the chants of the small contingent of the visitors' supporters. Even if I had not known that a small wedge of seating in one corner was reserved for the West Brom fans, it would have been obvious in the instant Arsenal slotted the first of what would be five goals. The stadium erupts in a bobbing, jumping, screaming mass of humanity around its entire circumference except for that one-sixteenth slice, which remains resolutely, humourlessly motionless. Delirious with joy, the 40,000 supporters of the home team point, as one, at the still, silent wedge of seating, bellowing (the tune is the *Bread of Heaven* refrain from *Guide Me, O Thou Great Redeemer*): 'You're not cheering. You're not cheering. You're not cheering any more.'

The sight is even more comical, when West Brom scores in the second half and the proportions are reversed. Watching, I feel like a zoologist examining a new and strange form of life. I want to fit in here because I sense it's my birthright, the fulfilment of some part of my destiny. But what is unfolding in front of me seems as strange as a Masai initiation ritual.

There's a man across the room staring at a large computer monitor and singing at the top of his lungs.

'Panties and thongs,' he sings. 'Panties and thongs, knickers and panties and panties and thongs.'

He seems a nice enough chap, and he's inspired by what's in front of him: a page layout on the computer which shows a busty woman dressed in nothing else but one pair of the pieces of lingerie that so inspire him. He's in charge of the words that will hold the picture up – an essentially meaningless snatch of racy prose that personalises the well-built woman, whose name is almost certainly Kimberly – so that readers will feel like she is real, rather than a performer in a media circus called the *Sun*.

The headquarters of the biggest-circulation newspaper in the English-speaking world (at almost 3.75 million, it dwarfs America's biggest, *USA Today*) are on the edge of the Thames at Wapping, just east of Tower Bridge. And for the folks on the *Sun*, big means best. Above the swing door leading onto the editorial floor are emblazoned the words: 'Hold your head up. You're entering the offices of the world's greatest newspaper.'

This is where Australian owner Rupert Murdoch moved to when in the 1980s he decided to break the powerful print unions by sacking them all and relocating to new headquarters, whose impregnability quickly earned it the nickname Fortress Wapping. There he taught non-printers – in his case, he retrained electricians – to typeset on computers. The move presaged the quick end of Fleet Street as other proprietors followed suit. The papers' offices were scattered all over inner London, on the south side of the Blackfriars Bridge and further into the Docklands at Canary Wharf.

The derisory value of the New Zealand dollar has forced me to look for a few days' work on a newspaper here and the *Sun*, whose features editor is quick to offer me a few shifts as a sub-editor, seems a good place to test the water.

A sub-editor, or 'sub', is not – as many outside the business seem to think – a deputy to the editor. Sub-editing or 'subbing' involves taking the copy provided by reporters, which has been passed by the news editor, and making it fit into predetermined layouts of the pages. In the old days of hot metal, this was accomplished by a keen instinct for 'casting off' – estimating the number of lines in a given column width a given piece of typed copy would fill. Fine adjustments to the fit were accomplished on the stone – much of the terminology of newspapers dates back to the primitive printing rooms of the monasteries in Caxton's England – where the printers worked to the subs' instructions.

Well that's how it was meant to happen. In practice, the 'stone sub', who works alongside the printers, was a solo operator in an alien territory and would do anything to keep on the right side of them. In my early years, I would often file late-night theatre reviews; if they ran too long, the stone sub – consumed more by thirst, I suspect, than the desire to see that the writer's intentions were reflected in the next day's paper – would ingratiatingly instruct the printer to slice off the last paragraph.

When the excision had skewed the balance of a review once too often I complained to the news editor, who issued instructions that reviews were not in future to be blithely cut from the bottom. The next time a review of mine appeared, the penultimate paragraph had been surgically excised. The fact that the final paragraph began with the word 'nevertheless' might have been a signal that this decision was perilous, but I am sure that malice, rather than carelessness prompted that decision.

Virtually my entire professional life having been spent on a sober, even staid, broadsheet, the decision to work on the *Sun* may be compared to heading into tiger country. The others on the features bench are welcoming enough. They're used to casuals from the antipodes showing up – the first two I speak to are an Australian couple from Bourke in far western New South Wales. And the work is menial, exacting rather than taxing. Mostly it involves checking details, making sure that published phone numbers and websites are right by ringing or visiting them or confirming that *The Man Who Shot Liberty Valance* was, as the film critic says, released in 1962 and directed by John Ford.

For a writer it's a bit galling. And when there is a chance to write, it's essentially a process of emulsifying copy from various sources – unadorned press releases or the copy of kids barely out of adolescence – into the house style: 'The *Sun* is giving you the chance to rock your socks off in fabulous Ibiza. All you have to do is ...'

Most of the reporters couldn't read or even walk when I started in journalism; as far as I can gather one of the major qualifications for working here is to tote a snappy briefcase (men) or totter on elegant heels (women) and say 'All right?', pronouncing the final 't' as a glottal stop, instead of the now passé 'Hello'. And it's vital to be young, with a face unravaged by the lines people get when they think about what they are doing.

A chap in charge of a lifestyle page swings by the subs' desk wondering aloud at the meaning of the word 'Zeitgeist' and flicking aimlessly through the dictionary, presumably because he's not entirely sure what letter it begins with. I feel faintly old-fashioned for thinking that a lifestyle editor shouldn't have to ask that question – the word presumably doesn't come tripping from the tongues of the *Sun*'s readers on a daily basis, after all. But mainly I feel impatient when, having told him its meaning, I explain where it came from and why and he doesn't even pretend to be interested.

But if the reporters' benches look like a kindergarten, the subbery is more like an old folks' home. This is journalism's Jurassic Park, but the dinosaurs are not cloned and recreated. They have survived Murdoch's purges and they are the proud standard-bearers of a noble tradition of English – indeed, Commonwealth – journalism: drinking heavily during working hours.

The classic is a man everyone calls Steady, a florid chain-smoking veteran of 40 years in the business. At 8.30 p.m. when the first edition is away, he leads the rush for the Old Rose up on the Highway. It's called the dinner break but the food here consists of peanuts and crisps and nobody eats. Here Steady and a hard core of the old troops pour liquor down their throats with a frightening speed and sense of purpose.

I make a grander entrance than I'd intended when I arrive to find they've already bought a pint for me. I sit down and my knee violently knocks the table leg, sending the beer rushing in a foamy tide across the tabletop. Subs scatter and I take several nights – and some pretty careful navigation – to live it down.

When I tell them after the third pint that I've had enough – being able to focus on small print is a bit of a bonus on the job, I reason – they look at me as though I'm mad. When I look at my watch and wonder if it wasn't time we wandered back, they cry out in an injured unison, 'There's another three minutes yet. Whose round is it?'

Steady spends his whole time grumbling about his working conditions, which comprise a four-day week, subsidised health care, a cheap and good canteen and a salary that, as far as I can gather, is more than £50,000 a year – roughly what a professor at a high-end university might expect. He owns a house in Marbella on the Costa del Sol and regularly arranges his work weeks so he has six-day weekends when he takes off to his Spanish hideaway on £29 flights whose cost he easily recoups in savings made on duty-free cigarettes and liquor.

For all that, I enjoy spending time with these men. The liquor flows warmly through my veins and I enjoy listening as they swap stories; since they seem singularly uninterested in mine, listening quickly begins to look like the sensible option. In an odd way, I yearn to be one of them.

I linger round London for a few weeks, feeling less like a tourist with each passing day and yet, paradoxically, less and less at home. The clouds of war, which will break into the American-led invasion of Iraq, are just beginning to gather. I feel a dull sense of anxiety, like a low-level constant alarm, at being near the geopolitical epicentre. I long to be back in the land on the other side of the world, far away from everything.

Yet, perversely perhaps, I resent the sense of New Zealand's invisibility over here. The lack of interest from the journos at the *Sun*, glowering into their dinner-time pints, started it. I was full of the visitor's curiosity, plying them with questions to which they seldom replied directly, instead icing the answer with a sly and knowing wink thrown in the direction of their workmates. It was not meant unkindly, but the effect was dismissive. 'You're not one of us,' it seemed to say, which was nothing if not accurate.

That they were so incurious about me was probably a measure of the isolationism that seems so typical of the Englishman at home. They knew where New Zealand was all right, and that it was the home of the All Blacks. Some had even heard of *The Piano*, a film which was set in New Zealand but was an Australian production financed by a Frenchman, though those who knew about our nuclear-free policy didn't much care about it. Beyond asking me where I lived and offering the interesting news that they had been to (or would like to go to) Australia, they seemed more interested in talking about the weekend's football.

I was soon to see their knowledge of basic Pacific geography as positively encyclopaedic. Newspapers published world maps showing different nations' attitudes to the Americans' sabre-rattling pronouncements about disarming Saddam Hussein; east of Australia was a wide expanse of empty ocean as far as the edge of the page.

It got worse. A walk-on world map outside the Natural History Museum in South Kensington likewise simply ignored our existence. Spread out over an area the size of a tennis court, it flattened the globe into a representation that dispensed with the part between longitudes 160 and 180 degrees east of the Greenwich meridian. Fuming, I stumped along to the reception desk and asked if they had a suggestion box. They did not – and did not seem especially taken with my suggestion that they install one. After several long moments of farting about, the young woman on duty came up with a piece of paper on which I was able to record my distress at having my country obliterated by an act of curatorial ineptitude. She took the paper from me and tucked it beneath her telephone. I have little doubt that, if she did not bin it before I disappeared from view, it is tucked there still.

On a warm Saturday morning, I take the train to Peterborough where David, with Mum in tow, drives to collect me. Mum, silhouetted in the front seat of the car as they pull up, looks small and frail. Her hand clasps the top of her seatbelt near the door pillar and it looks as though she is holding on for her life.

We drive through sunlit countryside to the small village near Oakham where they live. Their home sprawls like a Waikato farmhouse; it sits on an immaculate half-acre, which David mows with a ride-on. Inside, the house is full of the clutter of a life busily lived. Nooks are filled with different workspaces. The many bedrooms look regularly used and not like the shrines to now-distant children who last slept there in their teenage years.

It's a warm summer morning but Margaret, giving no sign that it is anything unusual, is preparing a boulder-size roast of beef with all the trimmings – Yorkshire pudding and half a dozen kinds of roast vegetable. For a flickering moment, as my mind processes the crisp and mouth-watering scent of the slightly charred skin of fat on the roast, I fancy she's set the menu to make us feel at home. Whether it was her intention or not, we do – here in the heart of Leicestershire I might as well be in Hamilton.

We linger over port and David discusses his plans for Mum. He has plainly slaved over the itinerary for weeks. Each day is planned in minute detail. Routes are plotted to the hour. Places where they will stop for morning tea are even specified.

I am gobsmacked by the planning he has put into everything and feel a sharp stab of regret that I had not taken Mum's itinerary for our trip down south in hand to ensure that our last day there – and her memory – would not be clouded with sighs of disappointment.

For all his fussy precision, David is as interesting as he is hospitable. He's retired now from a distinguished career as an optical engineer – only a year ago he was awarded the Konrady Medal, the Nobel Prize in the field, for a lifetime of work that included designing the lens system for photocopiers. It makes him an endlessly fascinating interlocutor.

As we talk, Mum's persistence in remarking of anything mentioned that 'We have that in New Zealand' begins to get on my nerves. In London where she had wondered whether they stole John Logan Campbell's epitaph for Sir Christopher Wren, it had been faintly comical, perhaps because I was the only person listening. Here I cringe with the embarrassment of a young boy whose mother has lumbered into the classroom with the lunch he forgot to pack in his schoolbag.

David is describing the acoustics of a concert hall in Birmingham, when the dam of my irritation finally bursts. It boasts an angled ceiling, he says, which reflects the sound out into the audience. Better still, the entrance doors around the auditorium's circular perimeter can be thrown open, allowing the concourse to be a massive resonating chamber. The design, the scientific mind enthuses, is singularly adaptable to the nature of the performance: closed down tight it provides the intimate setting for the smallest chamber ensemble and it can be thrown open to create an arena for Mahler or Beethoven in full throat.

'We've got that in the cathedral in Auckland,' Mum says, nodding knowingly.

'We do *not* have that in the cathedral in Auckland!' I explode. 'Why don't you just listen for a change instead of telling us that you have seen it all before!'

'I was only saying …' Mum begins, but I am into second gear.

'Nobody's interested in what you were saying. Just listen.'

The atmosphere at the table is suddenly electric. In David and Margaret's silence I fancy I can detect a slightly embarrassed sense of solidarity, as if I have given violent voice to something they may often have thought but are far too polite to say. They begin to clear the table and I, doggedly pushing through the waves of feeling that I have unnecessarily humiliated Mum and disgraced myself, hasten to help.

Later we visit Peterborough where David and I browse in an excellent bookshop full of first editions and I fight the temptation to buy a suitcase-load. When we leave the shop Mum has disappeared and we spend 20 minutes walking up and down the narrow streets looking for a glimpse of her before she reappears, squinting upwards at the rooftops. I upbraid her none too gently for not telling anybody where she was going.

'Give your mum a hug,' she says, her lower lip trembling. 'I feel rotten.'

'Why do you feel rotten?' I ask disingenuously.

'You know,' she says. But I brush her aside.

I am angry at myself for getting angry with her and angrier still at her for making me so angry. The feelings gather in a self-firing spiral, shame at my petulant adolescent outburst piling on the rage. I feel that my mother is not as interesting and interested as these distant relatives beside whom we seem so coarse and provincial.

In a moment, the whole sweet dream of the trip has imperceptibly crossed into sourness. I can't summon the grace to apologise for giving a tongue-lashing to someone who was simply trying to keep up with the conversation, trying to tame the welter of new information coming at her by relating it to something she did know. Unable to rise above the embarrassment of the small boy unwelcomely delivered his lunchbox in the classroom, I behaved like a spoilt and ungracious child. Ruefully, I wonder who is the more cringing colonial: the mother who spoke of the cathedral back home or the son who insisted that no attitude other than rapt and impressed attention was possible.

Mum sees me off at the station. Unable to look at the hurt in her eyes, I hug her and mutter some advice about keeping her eyes open and enjoying what is happening around her. It is a clumsy attempt to cover up my embarrassment by patronising her.

I mooch around London for a few more days, trying to set up meetings with David's two children, John and Elizabeth. Both are working in high-powered jobs – he in personal investment for one of the big banks, she in health-care policy development – and I begin to realise I should have made appointments months before. Only now, as my time is running out, do I begin to realise that I am fascinated by these people since they are what I might have become.

In the end, I cannot connect with Elizabeth; professional and family responsibilities are taking her out of town, and there is literally not even a lunch hour free before I leave.

John is easier to pin down. I wait as requested in the foyer of his building, next to the old Royal Mint and overlooking the Tower. I am expecting a sleekly suited corporate type, but he emerges in an open-necked checked shirt and carrying a small and rather tattered gym bag, which is not – he chuckles at the very thought – for his gym gear but 'my briefcase'.

We cross the Highway, along which I walked to and from the subbery at the *Sun* and drink real ale in a dark pub with newly varnished floors. John seems a long way from what I imagined as a corporate banking type. Most of his time, he says, is spent making sure that no one realises that he has no idea what he is doing. I am sure he doesn't mean it literally – there is too much of a sparkle in his eye for that to be the case – but he seems far less excited than his father by the fact that he is a multimillionaire in his mid-thirties.

Looking at John as he talks – confident, handsome, mischievously self-deprecating – I try hard (and fail) to see a family likeness. Raised in dank wintry Leeds, he should be a lugubrious, humourless Yorkshireman, whining about the weather. But the face that peers over the rim of the pint glass is clear and smiling. He dawdles over his pint, a pile of banknotes on the bar in front of him from which the barman picks what he needs when it is John's round. I, mindful of how many New Zealand dollars each £6 round is costing, nervously gulp my drink and feel more than ever out of place.

For the first time since I have been there, London is no longer a place of adventure and novelty but another tiresome foreign city where people do things differently. John and I, who have at least some shared blood flowing in our veins, seem separated by more than just the generations. He is an Englishman; I am not and never have been.

I ring Mum at David's before flying to Amsterdam, but there is no reply. I've long planned a visit to Berlin, but a Colin McCahon retrospective has just opened at the Stedelijk Museum and I can't resist a peek at the iconic New Zealand painter in such foreign surroundings. So I decide to fly to Holland and take the train across to Berlin.

The hot-dog stand outside the museum is selling coffee but spelling it 'koffie'. The streets, broken by curved bridges across ancient canals, are full of trams and bicycles. But inside, the walls are full of imagery from the other side of the world.

There they are: the glowering hillsides; the melting, aching faces; the runic arrangements of numbers, Arabic or Roman, backgrounded by ghostly landscapes; and everywhere that familiar rounded, upright handwriting and words full of longing and wonder.

Seeing the familiar (and many unfamiliar, long-unseen) works on the other side of the world is a bracing experience. It is like looking at them with fresh eyes; and they exert a powerful visceral tug, in the same way as the haka performed on foreign soil makes the neck-hair bristle more than normal.

The sight of one particular North Otago landscape fills me with such a sense of place and pride of ownership that I feel like crying out to the other patrons: 'This is my country, this. And this is exactly what it looks like, too.'

Seen so far from home, the landscapes seem to possess a haunting, almost photographic realism. In that environment the paintings are still full of mystery but quite without obscurity, postcards from the edge of the earth and from a place called home.

I am nagged by the sense that Mum is due to fly back any day. It has always been arranged that she will return alone, since I am staying on, and I know she will be anxious. David and Margaret will be seeing she is checked in and looked after and I keep reassuring her that Nicolas, the faithful Filipino, or someone equally competent will be there to help her through the layover in LA. Still, I know that the return will be a challenge even for someone who can now regard herself as something of a veteran traveller. And anyway, I want to say goodbye.

I keep trying David's home and mobile numbers without success. At last, about to board the train for Berlin, I ring my brother back in New Zealand.

'Sorry to cause a bother, but I can't seem to raise Mum,' I say. 'Have you heard from her?'

'She's fine,' he says, plainly not realising that I don't know I'd got the dates wrong and she's already flown. 'We gave her a cup of tea here and then took her home. She's tired, all right, but she's glad to be back.'

I hang up the phone in the hotel booth and go to the desk to pay for the call. I feel irrationally but intensely miffed that she has left without saying goodbye, even though she could hardly have done so since she had no idea where I was.

I step out into the watery sunlight and turn down the road towards the station.

HOME FROM SEA

Well, home is the Sailor, and that is a chapter
In a schoolbook, a relevant yesterday
We thought we knew all about, being much apter
To profit, sure of our ground.
– Allen Curnow, 'Landfall in Unknown Seas'

The cool of autumn is beginning to roll across the land as I head south. It's almost Easter and the Hauraki Plains stretch across to Mt Te Aroha, the largest of those blue remembered hills. We climbed it once, or meant to, I can't remember which. Memory is like that. You remember what you want to be true rather than what necessarily was.

I turn north at Kopu, heading for my brother's place near Tapu. Ngarimu Bay is on the way. It always seemed miles away to young boys in the back seat, anxious to arrive, but now it is only a few minutes north and I'm just finishing the ice cream I bought at Thames when the road dips slightly and the small bay surprises me.

I pull off onto the narrow shoulder of grass and stare at the bach. It's fenced off from the road now, protecting the occupants' children from the traffic that tears past only a few metres from the door.

The fibrolite is painted garish pink and the newish aluminium joinery has defaced the once simple lines with jutting faceted windows, replacing the louvres of what was built as a boatshed. The outside safe on the south wall, which used to keep the butter cool through those hot summers, has gone. The curtains are drawn. Unfamiliar, the place seems stripped of memory, and I resist the temptation to curse the owners for their carelessness.

We spend our early lives running from our past, keen to outdistance things we want to forget. Then our children begin to grow and start running from theirs. They might make a disparaging comment or two about the way we have lived our lives and suddenly our past seems more important, part of our definition of ourselves.

I spend the weekend before Easter on a marae near Katikati where a friend has invited me to a function to launch a CD of Maori music she has produced and performed. Elaborate mihi (greetings) and poroporoaki (farewells) bookend the celebrations. Guests stake their claim to being there by detailing their histories, describing their links to the hosts, to other guests, and to each other.

In my faltering Maori, I stumble through a short mihi before resorting to English. I speak of the sense I feel – a mixture of wonder and envy – of my disconnection from what is going on. Writing this book, I tell them, is a process of learning about my own history. But I don't have to go far back upstream to find that the flow of identity dries up or that the many small trickles of tributaries become indistinguishable from each other.

This is not to mourn the way we are; there is no point in that. But even with Geoff's book as a guide and after my own travels with my mother, my family remains a group of shadowy, mysterious figures. The living ones we meet only at funerals where our attendance is an expiation of having missed weddings and birthdays and other festivities to which we were anyway not invited. The dead ones struggle into fitful life on the page, but most of what animates them is the writer's imagination and not observable or verifiable fact.

The land endures. The landscape through which I drive back from the Bay of Plenty is indisputably mine. It touches my heart in a way England's green and pleasant land never did and reminds me of the photorealistic McCahon at the Stedelijk Museum and the lump it brought to my throat. I feel at last more here than before I went away.

Mum does, too, you can tell. She denies it, scoffs and feels faintly patronised when all her four sons say that she seems somehow calmer and more centred than before. Who knows if she found what she went looking for or if she was even looking for anything.

Maybe she was, as she always insisted, happy to just admire

that tree, this thatched roof, the age of the ancient cobbles.

'Been there, done that,' she laughs when I raise the subject with her. 'It was very nice and I'm very grateful. I still wish I'd been born there because that's where my blood is, where my heart is. But I don't feel in exile here. I'm a New Zealander, but I'm an *English* New Zealander.'

It's easy to pick holes in such a definition of herself, but who's to say it's wrong. The Englishness remains, but more pressing still is the need to learn 'the trick of standing upright here'. The rest is the past. And the past – so runs the famous line – is another country; they do things differently there.